MENTAL-SPIRITUAL HEALTH MODELS:

An Analysis of the Models of Boisen, Hiltner and Clinebell

Hugh W. Sanborn

University Press of America™

University Press of America, Inc.™
4710 Auth Place, S.E., Washington, D.C. 20023

Printed in the United States of America

ISBN: 0-8191-0784-0
Library of Congress Number: 79-65295

To

Barbara, Elisabeth and Daniel

With

deep gratitude for

their patience, love and

understanding without which this

study could not have

been completed

TABLE OF CONTENTS

Page

Page

LIST OF FIGURES

PREFACE

What is mental health? What is salvation or spiritual health?[1] How are they related? How are they to be understood or conceptualized from the standpoint of pastoral psychology and theology? What is entailed in developing a model of the nature and relation of mental and spiritual health? Through a comprehensive analysis of the mental-spiritual health models of three pastoral counseling specialists--Anton Boisen, Seward Hiltner and Howard Clinebell--the author attempts to draw the reader into an examination and critical evaluation of the model-building task within pastoral psychology and theology. More specifically, the purpose of this study is to make explicit the following: (1) the problems and issues[2] as well as strengths entailed in Boisen's, Hiltner's and Clinebell's treatment of their mental health-salvation models; and (2) the mental health-salvation model resulting from serious consideration of the directives emerging from the analysis.

A brief word about the scope of the study is needed lest the author's reasons for including a chapter on the background of the investigators be misconstrued. The present study attempts neither to provide a thorough biography of Boisen, Hiltner and Clinebell nor an evaluation of their various contributions to the field in general. With regard to the former, only that biographical material which serves to introduce these men to the reader and which is germane to the inquiry is presented.[3] Material pertaining to the intellectual background and orientation of these investigators is considered of particular importance for disclosing the frames of reference from which the models have been developed. With regard to the latter, only those contributions directly pertinent to the development and/or shape of the models are treated in this study.

Some readers may wonder why Boisen, Hiltner and Clinebell have been selected for this study. There are several reasons: (1) these pastoral psychologists/theologians have maintained that the explication of the concepts of mental health and salvation are of major significance; (2) they represent different though overlapping periods and trends in the pastoral care movement; (3) they themselves have been committed to the type of analysis and dialogue herein presented. Other contributors also meet these criteria.[4] However, Boisen, Hiltner and Clinebell lead their respective generations in terms of the scope and significance of their contribution in this area.

What separates Boisen, Hiltner and Clinebell from other contributors, then, is the status each has attained as a major contributor. They did not have to be singled out, for they already stand out among their colleagues. Boisen has been widely acclaimed to be one of the clinical fathers of modern pastoral psychology and theology.[5] In the judgment of Wayne Oates, Boisen's contribution in the area of religion and health is of greater significance than that of William James.[6] Hiltner, a student of both Boisen and Wise, stands alone in terms of both the quantity and quality of his writings during the past thirty years. He has exerted greater influence on the field during this period than any other man, a status for which he has been and continues to be highly respected and honored.[7] Clinebell, youngest of the three and indirectly a student of both Boisen and Hiltner, has established himself in recent years as a major influence on the field.[8] At present he is the leading contributor of his generation.

The origins of this study are rooted in the author's training and focal interests. Not dissimilar to the academic and clinical training of Boisen, Hiltner and Clinebell, the author has participated in clinical training in a mental hospital, specialized in pastoral counseling, and developed some of the same focal concerns centering in the health-promoting nature of Christian ministry and community. In this author's view from within the academic field of Religion and the professional field of ministry, both from a theoretical standpoint and practical standpoint, the focal issue for pastoral psychology and theology is how mental and spiritual health are to be approached and understood. In short, this study has sprung in part out of the author's particular interest in the nature and relation of mental health and salvation held in common with Boisen, Hiltner and Clinebell.

Furthermore, this study has been encouraged by the present lack of conceptual clarity with regard to the nature and relation of mental health and salvation. Most modern pastoral counselors carry out their work with at least a minimum of theoretical and practical understanding of what they mean by these terms. Few, however, have worked through the issues entailed in conceptualizing the nature and relation of mental and spiritual health from the standpoint of pastoral psychology and theology. Thus, on the level of conceptual understanding, there appears to be a considerable gap between the theoretical studies of pastoral specialists and the general orientation of pastoral counselors. This study arose from the author's recognition of the fact that what has been conspicuously lacking, that which would help bridge the existing gap, is an analytical discussion of the models themselves.

Pastoral counselors are not unique in this regard. Counselors in other fields have also lacked conceptual clarity with regard to mental health,[9] and few have explored the relation of ultimate questions to mental health. Nevertheless, some hopeful trends have become visible. Widespread recognition in recent years of the inadequacy of the statistical concept of normality as a synonym for mental health[10] together with dissatisfaction in many quarters with negative definitions--i.e., health defined in one way or another as the absence of illness--have tended to have two significant effects on those in the counseling field. They generally have led to an increased awareness of the problem's complexity, and they have brought about a renewed interest in the relevance of values to the problem.

No doubt due to the controversial nature of any consideration of values, no one model of positive mental health has been generally accepted.[11] The only thing generally acknowledged today is the interdisciplinary nature of the problem. This study, then, is a response to the stressing need of pastoral counselors to clarify what they mean by mental and spiritual health and thereby contribute to both the discussion within pastoral psychology and theology and the interdisciplinary dialogue.

The book is primarily addressed to pastoral counselors, clinical pastoral educators, seminary students and clergymen interested in pastoral psychology and theology, and graduate students in Religion and Personality, and secondarily to those in other helping professions who are interested in the nature and relation of mental and spiritual health.

Apart from a few minor changes, the analysis herein presented is the same in form and substance as it appears in the author's doctoral dissertation. Some consideration was given to including the most recent and significant contribution in the field, the mental health-salvation model presented by James Lapsley--see footnote 4. However, rather than burden the reader with an additional model, the author has decided to leave that task to those who find the method herein employed worthwhile to pursue.

Last but by no means least, the author is indebted to a number of persons for their various contributions to his development and present research in pastoral psychology and theology. Professors John Billinsky, Henry Brooks and the late Nels Ferre are among those who aroused the author's initial interest in this field during seminary years. Professors David Belgum and George Paterson of Iowa University provided assistance during the early stages of the analytical work. Their insightful questions, thoughtful criticism and helpful suggestions provided the kind of stimulation needed to get the analysis underway. Dr. Seward Hiltner and Dr. Howard Clinebell took time out from their busy schedules to read introductory portions of the manuscript and suggest pertinent changes. Finally, the personal and departmental support provided by Dr. Niels Nielsen, Chairman of the Rice Department of Religious Studies, assured the completion and publication of the study.

Among those who provided assistance in the technical preparation of the book are Constance Williamson, Josephine Monaghan and Maymee Meeks. Constance Williamson gave generously of her time and talent in preparing the diagrams, and Josephine Monaghan and Maymee Meeks demonstrated exceptional expertise as typist and proofreader of the manuscript, respectively.

To each of the above mentioned persons, and to my wife and children to whom this book is dedicated, the author extends his deepest appreciation.

Hugh W. Sanborn

Rice University

INTRODUCTION

Before the exploration gets underway, it perhaps will be helpful to introduce the reader to the method employed in the analysis, the author's use of the term "model" and the useful schema of models provided by Thomas Fawcett.[1]

Basic Method

The primary method followed in this study is that of general analysis or exposition. Each mental-spiritual health model is subjected to an analytical inquiry in an effort to discern the nature of antecedents, methodological assumptions and intentions, actual structure and content, and the concomitant problems and issues. Once this is completed, the study is concluded with a brief constructive attempt to embody the directives emerging from the analysis.

Two analytical procedures are employed, one throughout the analysis and the other in a more limited capacity. The former procedure is that of comparison and contrast. It is employed to understand the significant similarities and differences in the models. The latter procedure consists of the application of the categories of models and their values, as defined by Thomas Fawcett, to the models herein treated. The categories of models are initially employed in Chapter II, and the value categories of models are treated in the final chapter.

Since one of the main purposes of this study is to gain an illuminating view of the problems and issues entailed in the mental-spiritual health models of Boisen, Hiltner and Clinebell, each chapter is organized from the standpoint of considering the positions of each with regard to the general questions raised. The alternate approach of treating each model separately was considered. Organizing the study in this latter way would have the advantage of focusing full attention on the shape of one model at a time. Some readers will undoubtedly conclude that the author should have adopted that course. Hopefully, however, others will agree with the author that the disadvantage of deemphasizing dialogue between the three models during the presentation of each outweighs its advantage.

The organizational approach herein followed, then, was selected because it fosters dialogue throughout and thereby facilitates the analytical procedure of comparison and contrast. In short, it relinquishes the vantage of viewing each model separately in order to gain the advantage of bringing into sharp focus the way each pastoral specialist treats the various aspects of the problem.

Models and Their Uses

As used in this study, the term "model" refers to the nature of the interpretive categories employed for understanding the concepts of mental health and salvation. The term implies a particular methodological approach which is based on certain assumptions. It implies, in other words, a particular way of looking at and understanding something, in this case the nature and relation of mental and spiritual health.

In chapter five of THE SYMBOLIC LANGUAGE OF RELIGION,[2] Thomas Fawcett first considers basic ways in which models can be differentiated and then discusses various types of values models are reputed to have. What follows is a paraphrasing of Fawcett's approach. His categories will be applied as interpretive tools later in this dissertation.[3]

The first differentiation Fawcett makes is between descriptive and analogical models. A descriptive model is purported to present a scale replica of either some actual thing or mental image. Whether of an actual or mental form, the model depicts it, though usually in smaller or larger proportion, as it would look if observed in its existing state. The only possible distortion, then, is that due to the difference in size. An analogical model, on the other hand, provides a way of thinking about something which is either impossible to observe or not clearly pictured by the mind as it would look if available for observation. Rather than attempting to provide a scale model of the actual thing, an analogical model attempts to communicate a correspondence with regard to certain structural properties or particular characteristics. It is assumed that some form of structural similarity exists between the model and that which it is employed to illuminate. An analogical model, then, provides a means of articulating what would otherwise remain inaccessible to verbal communication.

The second differentiation Fawcett makes is between limited-relevance and control models. A limited-relevance model is one which is found to be useful for throwing light on some particular thing. It is employed because of its explanatory capacity within a restricted context. Underlying all limited-relevance models is a control model or model employed as a universal. A control model is definitive of a fundamental interpretive approach for grasping reality. Fawcett uses the term "control" because such a model is determinative of all other models employed by the particular approach. Whether it is employed explicitly or implicitly, it is pervasive as is disclosed by the terminology being used. A control model is limited, however, in that it is only one fundamental approach to and thus never exhaustive of the whole of reality.

Fawcett prepares the ground for his third differentiation by distinguishing between the control models of science and religion. The physical world provides the control model for science, man being treated objectively as a physical thing in the same way as a tree or a stone. On the other hand, personal being or man's subjective nature provides the control model for religion. Fawcett emphasizes the point that an essential characteristic of the scientific control model is the elimination of that which is the essential characteristic of the religious control model, namely, man's subjectivity. In the case of the former, man is treated under physical categories or dehumanized and removed from the world; in the case of the latter, man is understood as a subject and the physical world is treated existentially or from the standpoint of man's involvement with it.

With this distinction clarified, Fawcett makes his third differentiation by drawing out the fact that scientific models are observer models and religious models are participator models. Observer models objectify and participator models subjectify. Observer models are shaped to explain, represent and predict observed phenomena, while participator models are shaped to enable man to view the universe and his personal being as related in a way that is existentially or subjectively creative and meaningful.

Though Fawcett also considers "symbolic models" as a basic category of models, it would appear to be more correct or consistent with his approach to include the symbolic as a value of models. He himself begins his discussion of "symbolic models" by stating that any model could be seen as having "symbolic value." Thus the term "symbolic" is not descriptive of a particular category of models. Rather, as with his other value categories, the functional and cognitive values of models, the term "symbolic" clearly refers to a particular type of value that any model regardless of category could be subjectively assigned. This author, then, will consider the symbolic as a value of models along with the functional and cognitive values.

A model comes to have symbolic value for man, according to Fawcett, when it evokes a subjective or personal response. The fact that any model may take on symbolic value is rooted in the reality of man's subjectivity. In other words, because man is a subject, any approach or orientation to the world tends to have significance on the personal level.

The functional value of a model focuses attention on what actually occurs when a model is employed. From the standpoint of functional value, the truth question is inconsequential. The primary question is whether or not the desired results are attained. For the models of both science and religion, then, the functional value of models is extremely significant. The function of scientific models is to yield information that will lead to prediction and control. The function of religious models is to provide man with an orientation to the universe that will be creative of meaningful life and living.

Fawcett points out that while theology has relied on analogical models since its beginning, modern science has only recently begun to overcome its dissatisfaction with the use of analogical models. This is taking place not only because the difficulty of attempting to construct descriptive models is being recognized, but also because functional value is attained with the use of analogical models.

The cognitive value of models shifts the focus to the truth question or the relationship models have to reality. Do those who employ models intend them to be viewed entirely as functional tools with no cognitive value? Fawcett points out that a number of investigators do maintain this position: a model's validity is exhausted by its functional significance. Unlike scientific models, Fawcett asserts, religious models no longer are of functional value if their cognitive value is denied.[4] Either reality actually does have a personal dimension answering to man's subjectivity, or man is turned in upon himself, i.e., the humanizing, meaning-generating relationship is denied if the Thou (God) side of the relationship is removed. Religious models intend, then, to have cognitive value or assert something fundamental about reality, the same reality scientific models find it functionally useful to objectify.

With this brief presentation of Fawcett's categories of models and values of models before us, the stage is set for their employment as interpretive categories later in this study.

CHAPTER I

BOISEN, HILTNER AND CLINEBELL: PERSONAL, PROFESSIONAL AND INTELLECTUAL DEVELOPMENT

Based on the obvious assumption that the mental health-salvation models presented by Boisen, Hiltner and Clinebell were not shaped in a vacuum, this chapter undertakes the initial task of considering the major forms of influence that contributed to the development of these three men. Brief attention will be given first to the socio-cultural context, followed by sections on the personal, professional and intellectual background of each contributor.

Socio-cultural Milieu of the Times

The lives of the three men considered in this study, representing the years from 1876 to the present, span a period marked by many of the rapid changes and developments that have shaped modern society. Boisen was born and brought up at a time when a new sense of vitality and expectation was just beginning to gain momentum in America. While the country was still attempting to recover from the animosity and divisiveness of the Civil War years, new breakthroughs and discoveries in nearly all avenues of human endeavor were beginning to fashion an optimistic outlook toward the future. It was a time of excitement and hope, a time when America's deeply-rooted faith in progress was reinforced by the forward leaps of science and industry. By the turn of the century, such things as numerous mechanical inventions, related improvements in sanitation, communication and transportation, the promising beginning of modern medicine and an expanding economy convinced many that America was on the verge of realizing a new age of human fulfillment.[1]

Though America's faith in progress reached a high peak, all was not progress. The rapid changes that were taking place produced complex socio-economic problems as well as technological breakthroughs, victims as well as the prosperous. Increased industrialization, accompanied by increased immigration and urbanization, resulted in conditions that contributed to such difficult problems as city slums, conflicting social patterns and values, racial, ethnic and religious prejudice, and labor-management discord. What was applauded as progress, in other words, was often accompanied by debilitating and/or denigrating consequences for those isolated from social, economic and political influence. The bloody strikes, riots and lynchings that took place during the last quarter of the nineteenth century testify to the fact that all was not well with American society.[2]

Violence was not only present in the streets prior to the turn of the century. It was also present in the treatment of those persons who, for one reason or another, found functioning in society too problematic.

At first glance it appears ironic that at a time when modern medicine was rapidly developing, the quality of treatment for the mentally ill was deteriorating. During the first half of the nineteenth century, a humanitarian therapeutic approach known as moral treatment had begun to replace such unsound medical practices as bloodletting. Environmental factors had been considered important in treatment, and emphasis had been placed on education of and interaction with the community. Considerable optimism with regard to cure had prevailed.[3] During the second half of the nineteenth century, however, a reversion to a predominantly custodial approach took place as optimism waned, increasing numbers of immigrant and poor patients resulted in overcrowded institutions, communities demanded that alienated persons be isolated from society, and medical preference for classification of diseases and research into organic causes tended to discredit moral treatment approaches.[4] Earlier attempts at overcoming the stigma attached to mental illness were erased as fear and repulsion dominated the public attitude and stereotyping reached new proportions. Under such conditions, abuses within many institutions increased while effective therapeutic treatment decreased. The result was too often disastrous for those who found themselves trapped in such depersonalizing environments.[5]

At the turn of the century, then, many complex problems confronted American society. Not only were the problems complex because they entailed rapid changes taking place in the external structure of society. They were also complex because they involved changes in attitudes, philosophies and approaches to life which were more often than not resistant to change. Nowhere was this more evident than in the realm of religion. Traditional Protestant Christianity, as one source of such values as progress and individualism, had tended to foster association of these values with faith in the divine supernatural order.[6] At a time when naturalism, through its close alignment with science, was gaining strength in universities and among educated persons in general, and at a time when it was becoming increasingly clear that social and economic controls were desperately needed, conservative Christians found themselves on the defensive.[7] Progress, individualism and even supernaturalism were being questioned by increasing numbers of persons inside as well as outside the faith. For conservative Christians, the changes they saw taking place appeared to undermine the beliefs and way of life they cherished and were determined to defend.

The split between conservative and liberal groups widened as science continued to gain momentum and as society became increasingly secularized. On the one hand, conservative groups tended to hold fast to traditional values and beliefs and to emphasize conversion and individual piety. On the other hand, liberal groups tended to stress the importance of reinterpreting Christian beliefs or understanding Christian principles in terms that would be relevant to the problems facing modern society.[8]

In contrast to conservative groups, liberal groups generally were convinced that scientific methods could help clear away the superstitious debris that made the front yard of faith so needlessly cluttered and unattractive to modern minds. As well as promoting the adoption of modern historical, literary and archeological methods for studying the Bible and church history, they also generally supported the study of religion by behavioral sciences. However, as the behavioral sciences placed more and more emphasis on purifying their empirical methods, it became increasingly evident that many significant questions pertaining to the nature of religion would not be adequately treated, if treated at all, by secular fields. The clinical pastoral movement, as conceived by Boisen, was intended to help fill this gap by training men in clinical research methods.[9] Though clinical education failed to develop as Boisen had hoped, focusing instead on training for pastoral ministry, it nevertheless has served to stimulate further interest in a variety of problems related to religion and health.[10]

Imbued both with the spirit of progress and with deep concern about the socio-economic problems of the exploited, the social gospel movement began gaining momentum toward the end of the nineteenth century. The social gospel developed as the answer of the liberal churches to the changes needed both in Christian perspective and in approaching society's problems. Adherents of this movement maintained that individual rights and progress, lest they unwittingly foster social evils, must be understood within the Christian context of social progress. Thus social salvation was confirmed as being as important as individual salvation, the goal being the actualization of the kingdom of God in what was considered to be a basically Protestant society. Since the kingdom was envisioned as a just and harmonious community, social and economic planning and controls were called for to assure all groups of a fair share of America's abundance.[11]

The social gospel movement, with its predominant anti-Calvinistic emphasis on God's immanence and man's capacity for good, reflected the optimism that dominated the period. It enjoyed its prime years during the first decade of this century and was already in decline by the time Hiltner was in high school and Clinebell was still in infant's clothes. The realities of W. W. I and the Great Depression together with the increasing tendency toward a pluralistic society tended to bring about disillusionment with this movement and liberalism in general. A theological shift took place corresponding to the prevailing mood of pessimism during the thirties, W. W. II and on into the cold war years. Neo-orthodoxy, focusing on man's sin and need of redemption, attempted to regain the critical perspective of faith in a transcendent God whose immanence is not so readily identified with the plans and activities of men. Liberalism was attacked and discredited for the naive optimism of its misplaced faith.[12]

Only in recent years has the air cleared enough for re-assessment of the principles of liberalism. While some have called for a neo-liberalism combining the strengths of both liberalism and neo-orthodoxy, other voices have warned against trends which might result in the pitfalls of the old liberalism.[13]

Increasing interest in all aspects of the problem of health has been one of the predominant trends of twentieth century America. The shape this interest has taken, however, has varied considerably. At a time when the social gospel movement was calling attention to the needs of the less fortunate in the name of Christian progress, psychiatrists oriented to Social Darwinism, supported by some members of the clergy, were calling for a different form of progress. As their early nineteenth century predecessors, these psychiatrists were interested in the relationship between environment and heredity. The major concern was not the individual, as had been the case with moral treatment, but rather protection of society from degenerate characteristics which, if not checked by isolation and sterilization, might substantially weaken the race. The fact that some states passed sterilization laws is indicative of the temperament of some communities during that period.[14]

The approach of the extreme Social Darwinists together with the state of the mental hospitals placed emphasis on moral issues, especially those related to the rights and responsibilities of individuals and society. At the same time most psychiatrists were committed to the organic viewpoint with regard to causation of mental illness, distracting attention away from psychological and sociological factors. The time was thus ripe for breakthroughs in the slow-moving reform movement and in the comprehension of man's mental problems. The success of Beers, positive reception of Freud in America, and establishment of Meyer's orientation at Johns Hopkins, occurring almost simultaneously, signaled such breakthroughs.[15] Add to these such early contributions as those made by social psychology, educational philosophy and psychology of religion, and it becomes clear that the momentum generated in the search for a more comprehensive and balanced view of man as a healthy individual and social being was considerable.

Subsequent developments and events have indicated that the forces contributing to this early momentum have had to continue to contend with difficult counterforces. Though mental health became a national priority at least by the forties,[16] many mental institutions are still in need of reform and a stigma is still attached to mental illness in the seventies. Though the importance of promoting positive mental health has tended to spawn interdisciplinary approaches to the problem at all levels, limited perspectives and exclusivistic attitudes in theory and practice still threaten to retard such efforts.

At present an increasing number of voices have been generating new momentum by attempting to move beyond old theoretical impasses.[17] Since their mental health focus is on social structure and the social context of learning and communication, it would appear that it can only be understood within the larger context of the general dissatisfaction with society's failure to make substantial progress in resolving basic social problems. It would appear, in other words, to be one significant expression of the new wave of social revolution and progressivism that picked up pace in the sixties in an effort to bring about liberating changes in all spheres of society.

As difficult as it is to gauge the present mood of American society, it would appear that a new optimism is just beginning to emerge from the early successes of the social revolution. Whether viewed from a religious or secular context, it appears to be a guarded, cautious and critical optimism, cognizant of the polarization of viewpoints with regard to social change, yet increasingly aware of the many resources being mobilized to bring about constructive change. In this sense, it appears to be an optimism more reality-oriented than that of the social gospel movement, a factor which, if this assessment is accurate, may well prove itself to be a major force in effecting social change.

Boisen's Personal and Professional Development

In his extraordinary autobiographical study OUT OF THE DEPTHS, after presenting the fairly eminent family backgrounds of his well-educated and successful parents, Boisen retraces the development of his conflict-laden life from his earliest recollections. He presents a picture of himself as the first child and only son, born in Indiana in 1876, who from an early age was troubled with a sex-oriented problem, painful losses and feelings of guilt and inadequacy. In his own understanding, his life provides a case study of the development of a schizoid personality and the painful struggle to attain a creative resolution of the underlying conflicts.[18] Five related themes run throughout his autobiography: (1) his religious faith, (2) his sexual problem and related self-image, (3) his difficulty accepting losses, (4) his idealization of his parents and later the woman he loved, and (5) his vocational struggle.

Boisen's Presbyterian background--his father became a Congregationalist--included both liberal and conservative influences. From his parents he learned to view science and religion as thoroughly compatible.[19] At his grandfather's house, where he spent most of his boyhood years, he experienced the more formal religious approach to life including daily family prayers and limited activity on Sundays.[20] Religion was, in short, part of Boisen's heritage, and it later became a vital personal resource as well as his vocational field.

The core psychological problem, as Boisen describes it, was his inability to accept, socialize and assimilate his sex drive. He apparently learned to associate punishment with sex from his parents' responses to his early experiences of stimulation and exploration.[21] Be that as it may, learning about sexual intercourse later proved to be an upsetting experience, and throughout his adolescent years the subject held terror and fascination for him. The result was an increasing preoccupation with sexual fantasies accompanied by an increasing sense of guilt and isolation from the important persons in his life.[22]

Boisen's conflict reached its first critical point the year following his graduation from Indiana University. On Easter morning of 1898 he cried out to God for help. He describes what took place as a conversion experience which brought relief to his troubled mind and led him to share his problem with one of his college professors whom he associated with his father. He never forgot the advice this man gave him, namely, to seek help from Christ and "some good woman."[23]

The relief Boisen experienced was temporary, however, and his continued struggle to deal with his sexual conflict is integrally interwoven with the other themes of his life. To what extent he was aware of the connectives is not always made clear in his autobiography. What is made clear is the fact that his predominant self-image, that of a weak "wretch" and "failure," was associated with his inability to assimilate his sexual drive and to realize the level of success he felt was expected of him.[24]

While Boisen is explicit about the fact that the loss of his father at age seven was a significant event in his life, the fact that he tells so little about his actual reactions at the time together with his subsequent inability to cope with losses raises the question of whether he ever worked through his real feelings toward his father. In light of his sexual conflict, his relationship with his parents and difficulty dealing with his father's death would suggest to the orthodox psychoanalyst that his root problem was an unresolved oedipal complex.[25] While it is impossible to assess whether or not such an interpretation is valid, the question of its validity, as will become clear later in this study, is not inconsequential to the assessment of Boisen's model.

In any event, the painful loss of his father at age seven apparently left Boisen stranded with feelings he could neither verbalize then nor later. It is clear from his autobiography that he never outgrew his need to idealize his parents. Though he recalls unhappy experiences in his relationship with his father in which the latter conveyed that he viewed his son as weak and unacceptable,[26] Boisen never states nor even infers that he ever felt angry toward his father or guilt feelings following his death. His idealization of his father was reinforced by the directive given at his father's memorial service to remember him "at his best."[27] Boisen held fast to that directive and, if the need to work through feelings in relation to his father was a significant part of his problem, he never conveys awareness of it.

In a similar way Boisen also idealized his mother and apparently transferred this idealization and concomitant feelings to the "some good woman" he found in Alice Batchelder.[28] His mother and Alice are pictured as all goodness and purity in contrast to his wretchedness. Throughout his long and futile attempt to convince Alice to save him through marriage, he never once suggests that Alice also may have had problems that interfered with their relationship.

During his college years, Boisen's personal problems took priority over such issues as vocation. He conveys the impression that he was attempting to follow the path his father had followed.[29] Since he was unable to find a teaching position following graduation, he delved into the study of psychology. When he finally began his teaching career, he found French literature to be too great a temptation to handle. His old problem intensifying again, he decided to change his vocation to forestry.

Boisen associates his decision to enter forestry and his subsequent decision to enter the ministry with devotion to his father's memory and adds, with regard to the latter decision, that his love for Alice--who was employed in a form of ministry herself--also influenced him.[30] Since Boisen envisioned the two of them serving together, Alice's rejection of his offer left him in despair. After attending Yale Forestry School, he worked with the Forest Service for two years prior to entering Union Seminary. In 1911, upon completion of his seminary training, he was ordained a Presbyterian minister.[31]

The vocational question still remained a problem for Boisen, however, until after the war years and his first hospitalization. Prior to W. W. I, he held a number of ministry-related positions within the Presbyterian and Congregational denominations. Following the war, after working for a short time with the Interchurch World Movement, he turned down a position with the Congregational Social Service Commission in order to return to the pastorate. Alice's continued rejection during this period together with his failure to find a suitable church apparently precipitated his first lengthy psychotic withdrawal that radically altered the course of his life. While still hospitalized, he decided that to continue with his plans to become a pastor of a church was no longer feasible. He decided instead to commit himself fully to the task of researching the problem of mental illness.[32]

Boisen was aware of the fact that he had come close to slipping into psychosis earlier in his life. He states that brief periods of abnormality were associated with all of the major transitions he had made.[33] In his view, he experienced his first psychotic episode just prior to entering seminary when, again entertaining the hope of marrying Alice, he again experienced rejection. This break did not last long, however, and he avoided hospitalization. His second psychotic withdrawal resulted in hospitalization from October, 1920 to January, 1922. He was acutely disturbed during the first few weeks of his hospitalization and again in March of 1921--he considers this his third psychotic episode--when he was scheduled for transfer to another hospital for psychoanalytic treatment.[34]

The years that followed this major hospitalization were creative years in which Boisen became established as a new breed of theological researcher and educator. During the two years immediately following his hospitalization, he attended Harvard to renew his studies in several fields, particularly psychology, and formulate his project for the study of the relationship between religious experience and mental illness. He also served on the staff of the Social Service Department at Boston Psychopathic Hospital during 1923-24. Once his studies were completed, Boisen became Chaplain at Worcester State Hospital where he initiated clinical training for theological students. In 1925, he accepted additional responsibilities as Research Associate at Chicago Theological Seminary. Due to a number of factors, including his teaching responsibilities at the seminary, he became Chaplain at Elgin State Hospital in Illinois in 1932, a position he held off and on until 1955 when he was appointed Chaplain Emeritus.[35]

During most of his years at Elgin State Hospital, Boisen maintained a part-time teaching load at Chicago Theological Seminary. In 1938, however, he was at the seminary full time to write, teach and carry out a study of Pentecostal sects, a project financed by the Congregational Council of Social Action and the Social Science Research Council.[36]

Though in later years Boisen did take some constructive steps to improve his relationship with Alice, he apparently never adequately resolved the deep-seated problems that had interfered with his goal of marrying her. At the time of both his mother's death in 1930 and Alice's death in 1935, he suffered brief psychotic withdrawals.[37] The latter, coming at age fifty-nine, was to be his final hospitalization for mental illness. No further psychotic episodes are reported between 1935 and his death thirty years later, a period during which all of his books and many of his articles were published.

Boisen's Intellectual Development

Boisen's inquiring mind and personal and vocational struggles provided strong motivation for study of various schools of thought. Under the guidance of George Coe, his Psychology of Religion Professor at Union Theological Seminary, he was introduced to a number of scholars who contributed significantly to his orientation. Coe made reference to such men as Dewey, Mead, Cooley, Royce, Hocking, Delacroix and McDougall, the latter a psychologist under whom Boisen later studied. Boisen was already acquainted with James since he had read THE PRINCIPLES OF PSYCHOLOGY the year after graduating from college,[38] but through Coe he was exposed to the other major contributors in psychology of religion.[39]

Coe's PSYCHOLOGY OF RELIGION proved to be a most significant study for Boisen primarily because it directed his attention to the social nature of religion. Coe moved beyond individualism(James) and naturalism(Leuba) in his assertion that "the real world of the modern man is nature <u>plus society</u> (his italics)."[40] Religion, he held, is a matter of personal-social discovery.[41] Coe's emphasis on empirical method in general and a functional approach in particular, his stress on development of the whole person, and his attempt to maintain a balance between the individual and society all contributed to his student's perspective.

Boisen, however, reacted strongly against certain trends he found in Coe's thinking. One such trend that appears to have irked Boisen, perhaps as much personally as theologically, was an element of Coe's liberalism.[42] Coinciding with the spirit of the times, the predominant theological tone of such studies as RELIGION OF A MATURE MIND is optimistic with regard to the state of Christian consciousness. Coe held that the level of Christian development--the context of his statements indicates he was referring to the liberal Christian community--generally had advanced to such an extent that the traditional issues of sin and salvation were no longer of primary concern.[43] He recognized the one-sidedness of his position and attempted to counter it by adding statements about "concrete evil," but such statements could not detract from the stark insensitivity a Boisen would readily perceive in Coe's recommendation to put evil out of one's mind.[44]

Coe's approach to the problem of evil in human life together with his conviction, shared by most of the psychology of religion investigators, that mental illness was not an appropriate subject for the psychology of religion, elicited strong criticism from Boisen.[45] In light of the findings of early studies which, Boisen noted, tended to contradict the latter viewpoint, continuing to maintain such a position could only be viewed as irrational.[46] The presence of pathology is no valid reason, Boisen argued, for ruling out the study of those persons who know well the meaning of evil and need of salvation.

It is clear that Boisen, though deeply indebted as he was to Coe, viewed Coe's orientation as lacking something for which he was searching. He returned to the sources of Coe's thought and later developed the leads he received from Coe within his own developing perspective.

It was William James who provided part of what Boisen had found lacking in Coe. The markedly different tone and approach of James's THE VARIETIES OF RELIGIOUS EXPERIENCE from any of Coe's studies conveyed to Boisen that James was neither unfamiliar with the deep pain and conflict suffered by the mentally ill nor willing to have psychology of religion draw an arbitrary line at the door of the mental institution. In James, then, Boisen found an investigator who recognized the significance of the problem of mental illness for the study of religious experiences. In THE VARIETIES, it is the religion of the sick soul which takes both evil and man's need for salvation seriously.[47] Furthermore, James stated explicitly that he only dealt with half of mysticism in his study of the religious mystics. "The other half has no accumulated traditions except those which the text-books on insanity supply."[48] Though James himself did not deal with psychotic cases, the implication that such a study might prove profitable did not escape Boisen.[49]

In THE PRINCIPLES OF PSYCHOLOGY, James pointed out that psychological questions lead to metaphysical questions which are beyond the scope of empirical method.[50] He also maintained the position, however, that narrow empirical method is inadequate for studying man.[51] Open inquiry which refuses to allow method to block research into any potentially productive sphere of human concern and experience is, in James's view, essential. The result in both THE PRINCIPLES and THE VARIETIES is the employment of a broad empirical method which includes a form of phenomenology in an effort to expose the fundamentals of human nature. In THE VARIETIES, James's phenomenology is implicit in his concluding hypothesis which attempts to bridge the gap between science and metaphysics:

> Whatever it may be on its farther side, the 'more' with which in religious experience we feel ourselves connected is on its hither side the subconscious continuation of our conscious life. Starting thus with a recognized psychological fact as our basis, we seem to preserve a contact with 'science' which the ordinary theologian lacks.[52]

In his hypothesis James focused attention on the significance of understanding the nature of the psychological side of what he called the 'more'. This way of looking at the problem of the nature of religious experience together with James's suggestive methodological assertion regarding what "the ordinary theologian lacks" provided Boisen with significant keys. What will become clear when Boisen's method is fully considered in the following chapter, is that Boisen began at this very point where James left off in THE VARIETIES.

Boisen's own methodology attempted to overcome two limitations he found in that of James. First, Boisen learned from Cabot that nothing could take the place of firsthand study of actual cases.[53] This he found lacking in James who made extensive use of autobiographical material. Second, James was similar to Freud in his overemphasis of the individual. Boisen chose to focus his criticism on Freud rather than James, no doubt in part because Coe's work already served as a corrective to James's individualism. It would also appear that Boisen ignored this in James because he recognized that his predecessor was fighting a different battle, that pertaining to the validity of religious experience. He could not ignore Freud's individualism, however, because he viewed Freud as failing to recognize the significant implications of his own findings.[54] Thus Boisen's criticism was mainly leveled at Freud though by implication included James.

Boisen also profited from the long-term controversy that took place between William James, Josiah Royce and John Dewey (among others) over the nature of truth and reality. Both James and Dewey maintained that the term "truth" only has meaning when it is understood in pragmatic terms as referring to consequences in experience or action.[55] An actual difference in principle would necessarily make an actual difference in experience. For James, this became one major frame of reference for considering the ultimate nature of reality or the God question. The world-view one embraces, he argued, makes a significant difference for one's life and living.[56] Dewey, on the other hand, became convinced that no constructive functional difference obtains between ideals and the traditional concept of the divine. The religious object, he eventually concluded, is a superfluous, intellectual substitute for ideals. He called for a demythologizing of ideals in order to clarify and focus on the important pragmatic task of transforming ideals into action.[57] For Dewey, then, the pragmatic method was wedded to naturalism, while for James it stressed the difference supernaturalism or the existence of God would make, if true, in actual living.

Royce, James's former student and colleague at Harvard, disagreed with the anti-absolutist position of James and Dewey. In Royce's view, the relative nature of the pragmatic understanding of truth renders it meaningless apart from its grounding in Absolute Truth.[58] Both James and Dewey argued in effect that such an approach, in its attempt to squeeze all of reality into a unified, closed, abstract system, is inconsistent with the major tenets of pragmatism. Philosophy, they insisted, must not be permitted to take the place of experience.[59]

The importance of avoiding sterile, meaningless categories by starting with concrete reality was considered to be essential by Boisen.[60] Here he was in full agreement with James and Dewey. However, neither James's nor Dewey's position seemed fully adequate for describing the processes he was studying. James's position, while cognizant of the potentially creative function of mystical experiences, failed to recognize the significant implications of social process for pushing back the veil from man's side of religious experiences. Dewey's position, closed to the evidence of mysticism, resulted in redirecting faith away from any transcendent source to man's intellect as the only adequate guide for social behavior. Boisen sought a descriptive term which would effectively bridge the individual and social spheres while pointing beyond man and his values. He found such a term in Royce's PHILOSOPHY OF LOYALTY.

Apparently, Royce had developed his concept of loyalty as a way of combatting the criticism of James and Dewey.[61] Loyalty, he contended, is embedded in concrete experience; it is a relative term with reference points in individual experience, social experience and the cause which lies beyond the individual.[62] As long as he developed his position from the standpoint of concrete loyalty or loyalty as it is operative in the lives of men, James and Dewey were silenced. The inevitable test came, of course, when Royce attempted to answer theoretical problems. He was forced to take refuge in the abstraction "loyalty to loyalty,"[63] thus exposing himself once again to the criticism he was attempting to avoid. The lesson was not lost on Boisen. Method was the real issue at stake, not the adequacy of Royce's pragmatic understanding of loyalty. Within the context of his own method, Boisen followed Royce in employing loyalty as a major descriptive concept.[64]

Another side of the disagreement between James and Dewey focused on the nature of religious experience. James had argued in THE VARIETIES that what makes an experience religious is the object of religion, not what takes place in the experiencer. Religion, he asserted, is only one thing that can bring about unity of the personality.[65] Dewey turned this around, maintaining that while anything can bring about a unifying experience, what is religious is the function rather than the cause.[66] Boisen, who agreed with Delacroix that the goal of all mysticism is personality transformation,[67] attempted to expose the element of truth in both positions by focusing on what is actually entailed in the unification process. What Royce attempted to explicate on basically Kantian philosophical grounds, i.e., that the human quest requires pre-existing conditions that transcend the individual, Boisen attempted to demonstrate in terms of the socio-psychological dynamics of man's unifying experiences.[68]

What no doubt has become apparent by the above discussion is the fact that Boisen, following Coe's lead, was deeply influenced by social psychology. Coe had been convinced by social psychologists that man is basically a social creature. If this still remained an open question for Boisen following his reading of Coe's PSYCHOLOGY OF RELIGION and study under Coe, then his own reading of Mead, Cooley and Dewey resolved the issue. Be that as it may, the basic approach of social psychology together with the implications pertaining to individual and social development played a predominant role in shaping Boisen's thinking.

As was implied earlier, it was Boisen's orientation to social psychology that largely shaped his criticism of Freud. Boisen was introduced to Freud during his first hospitalization at a time when he was seeking confirmation of his own insights.[69] He viewed Freud as breaking new ground on the same plot into which he himself was about to plunge his shovel. Following further study of Freud, his initial excitement waned, and he began to view Freud as falling short of the great potential his initial groundbreaking had promised. Boisen became disillusioned by the fact that Freud, devoting as much attention as he did to the relationship of religion to personality development, was so closed to the constructive function of religion.[70] While he continued to view Freud as "a great pathfinder"[71] and to acknowledge his contribution, Boisen assumed a critical posture which resulted in the rejection of many of Freud's conclusions, modification of a number of Freudian concepts, and avoidance of psychoanalytic terminology.

It should be noted that it was not long after his introduction to Freud that Boisen studied under William McDougall, Harvard Professor of Psychology, and C. Macfie Campbell, Harvard Professor of Psychiatry and Director of Boston Psychopathic Hospital. Boisen considered both men to be outstanding contributors in their fields.[72] Under McDougall, Boisen read more of Freud as well as studies by Jung, Janet and Meyer.[73] McDougall was interested in and less critical of Jung, especially during earlier years, than he was of Freud.[74] Campbell was enthusiastic about Jung's work and more responsive to Meyer's broad concerns than to the narrow focus of Freud.[75] Both of Boisen's Harvard professors, in other words, were less than satisfied with Freud's views and attracted by more inclusive constructive orientations.

The type of position promoted by these two professors found a ready recipient in Boisen. Following in the tradition of James, both McDougall and Campbell expressed interest in the relation of religious factors to human development. In Campbell, Boisen found a psychiatrist who was critical of all forms of reductionism and seriously attentive to the role values play in personality integration.[76] In McDougall, he found a psychologist who viewed psychology as a science of mind and who approached the mind from a purposive, dynamic orientation without neglecting the social environment. McDougall was concerned about some of the same issues which Boisen considered to be vital, and thus it is not surprising to find much of McDougall's psychology contributing to the shape of Boisen's position.[77]

Boisen also was attracted by the contributions of Jung and Rank and to some extent by the work of Meyer. The emphasis the latter placed on the patient's ideology impressed Boisen, but he found that Meyer had been inattentive to the significance of religious factors in mental illness.[78] Both Jung and Rank, on the other hand, recognized some of the basic religious issues involved in man's problems and were moving, in Boisen's view, toward a more profound understanding of the relationship of religion to mental illness than either Meyer or Freud.[79]

The results of Jung's study of neuroses and the related phenomenon of the unconscious deserved more careful consideration, in Boisen's assessment, than they had received up to that time. Boisen viewed Jung's clinical findings as moving beyond Freud's on four important issues: (1) Jung redefined libido as a term referring to psychic energy in general; (2) he interpreted the cause of one group of neuroses as due to repression of one's morality rather than negative elements of the personality; (3) he recognized that the symptoms of neuroses have a progressive as well as a regressive function; and (4) he identified and attempted to describe phenomenologically what he labeled the "collective unconscious"--what James apparently had referred to as the 'farther side'.[80] With regard to the second and third, Jung's analysis may have partially influenced as well as received support from Boisen's conclusions.[81] Regarding the fourth, Boisen pointed out that his own personal experience lent support to Jung's view of the collective unconscious.[82] Though Boisen was convinced that Jung's model of the unconscious provided a more adequate hypothesis than Freud's, it was still an hypothesis, and Boisen contented himself with treating it as such.[83]

Two other psychiatrists, Franz Alexander and Harry S. Sullivan, the former closer to Freudian orthodoxy at the time than the latter, particularly caught Boisen's attention through their publications. Alexander's understanding of guilt and his recognition of the predominant role of the need for punishment in neuroses coincided with Boisen's findings. It was Boisen's view, however, that Alexander failed to distinguish between the role of self-punishment in neuroses and its role in other forms of illness as well as in the healthy personality.[84] Some of Boisen's findings with regard to acute psychoses corroborated those of Sullivan. Though Sullivan published the preliminary results of his observations first, Boisen maintained that their conclusions were reached independently.[85]

Boisen's discovery of Sullivan led to considerable professional interaction as well as an enduring friendship. The two men concurred in a number of their views, including their understanding of the importance of interpersonal communication for personality development and the significance of the role of participant observer for research. On at least one public occasion, Sullivan verbally supported elements of Boisen's understanding of the relation of religion to mental health.[86]

The concept of emergent evolution is a fundamental theme in Boisen's comprehension of mental and spiritual health. Though the concept of evolution was part of the thinking of most of the men he read, it would appear from his own position that he was influenced primarily by the views of McDougall, Hocking, Sullivan, and W. A. White. His basic position appears to follow closely that of McDougall who, as Boisen, rejected the blind nature of Bergson's elan vital.[87] In MODERN MATERIALISM AND EMERGENT EVOLUTION, McDougall presented his arguments for the position that evolution only pertains properly to the organic realm, and emergent evolution only to "Mind." Emergents are the products of intelligent, goal-oriented activity--which is what McDougall meant by teleological causation.[88] There is nothing in Boisen's position which would dispute or contradict any aspect of McDougall's stance on this issue.

For Boisen, Sullivan and White from a psychiatric point of view, and Hocking from a philosophical perspective, complement the type of position elaborated by McDougall. White's application of the theory of emergent evolution to his understanding of the relationship between conflict resolution and mental integration[89] was very similar to the view adopted by Sullivan and Boisen. Boisen stated explicitly that he followed Hocking in the latter's basically Bergsonian conception of conscience as the highest emergent.[90]

From a theological standpoint, Boisen's pronounced dissatisfaction with abstract orientations and his explicit focus on human experience and social valuation place him in the tradition of Schleiermacher and Ritschl. Though Boisen never gives any indication of having read the major works of either of these theologians, he was familiar with their orientations through the two liberal seminary professors who appear to have influenced his theological thinking most, William Brown and Walter Rauschenbusch.

Boisen's criticism of all abstract forms of theology applied more to Brown, his theology professor at Union, than it did to Rauschenbusch. In his liberal, Ritschlian-oriented Christocentric theology, Brown attempted to synthesize Schleiermacher's emphasis on experience with elements of the speculative and dogmatic traditions.[91] One result of Brown's method was that he focused primarily on Christ's experience and only secondarily on the experience of modern men.[92] While Boisen rejected such an approach, it would appear that he considered a number of the issues with which Brown dealt to be of no little importance.[93]

What apparently attracted Boisen to Rauschenbusch, Professor of Church History at Rochester Theological Seminary, was the latter's attempt to awaken theologians to the social nature of Christianity. The task that absorbed Rauschenbusch, which he viewed as promoted by such predecessors as Schleiermacher and Ritschl,[94] was bringing about a transition from the traditional individualistic theology to a sociologically relevant theology. Within this context, he stated: "Theology ought to be the science of redemption and offer scientific methods for the eradication of sin."[95]

Rauschenbusch's CHRISTIANITY AND THE SOCIAL CRISIS, which was published the year before Boisen entered seminary, was "an epoch-making statement of the social gospel," according to Boisen.[96] In this study, following his historical interpretation of what the Church should have but often had not maintained as its central purpose--i.e., transformation of society into God's kingdom--Rauschenbusch called attention to the interrelationship between the regenerated personality and social process.[97] In his THEOLOGY FOR THE SOCIAL GOSPEL, he developed this theme further in his attempt to disclose the nature of sin and salvation in concrete experience.[98] Both Rauschenbusch's insights pertaining to the nature and significance of Christian social process and his view of what "theology ought to be" appear to have contributed to the fermentation process going on within Boisen during his seminary and post-seminary years.

Hiltner's Personal and Professional Development

Born in Pennsylvania in 1909, Seward Hiltner was the oldest of his parents' two sons. In marked contrast to the difficult, preoccupying struggles Boisen experienced from an early age, Hiltner recalls a happy childhood with only the tightness of money creating a minor problem. He was an outgoing, energetic boy who, as well as holding part-time and summer jobs from about age ten, found time to learn to play two musical instruments and participate in various sports.[99]

Hiltner conveys that his mother more than his father has been a major influence in his life. While he briefly describes his father as a lower middle class worker and avid gardener, he describes with pride his mother's considerable ability and success as a writer.[100]

The religious community in which Hiltner's family belonged was, in his words, "more moralistic and pietistic than it knew."[101] Hiltner states that his own parents--especially his mother--were theologically literate and open to discussion of issues even when their son's questions troubled them. The predominant theological posture of the community, however, tended to place pressure on children to prepare for the experience of conversion. As early as age eight, Hiltner recalls, he felt this kind of pressure, but not even the appeals of a visiting evangelist seven years later could overcome his resistance to such an approach.[102]

Hiltner reached his decision to pursue a ministry-related vocation while he was still in high school. Realizing that he would not be able to earn sufficient funds to cover the expense of college, he added special tutoring to his list of activities in preparation for competitive scholarship exams. The fact that he won two scholarships was predictive of the kind of success he went on to achieve in his studies. After graduating summa cum laude from Lafayette College in 1931, he enrolled at the Divinity School of the University of Chicago for graduate study in theology. Though he completed his Ph.D. comprehensive exams in 1935, he did not feel the need to complete degree requirements until some fifteen years later.[103]

After his initial quarter of clinical pastoral education, which he took the summer of 1932, Hiltner was convinced of the value of this form of training. He took two more quarters the following two summers.[104] In 1935, the year of his ordination into the ministry of the Presbyterian Church, he put aside his graduate work and accepted the position of Executive Secretary of the Council for Clinical Training. During the three years that he served in this capacity, he established two more training programs, one at Pennsylvania Hospital in Philadelphia, and the other at the University of Michigan Hospital in Ann Arbor.[105]

Prior to the beginning of his full-time teaching career, Hiltner served as Assistant Minister to churches in Chicago and New York, and as Executive Secretary (1938-50) of the Department of Pastoral Services (Commissions on Religion and Health and on Ministry in Institutions), Federal Council of the Churches of Christ in America. After serving as Lecturer at Union Theological Seminary and Yale University Divinity School from 1945-50, he accepted the position of Associate Professor of Pastoral Theology at the University of Chicago (1950-54), and the position of Professor (1954-61). In 1961 he joined the Princeton Theological Seminary faculty as Professor of Theology and Personality, the position he presently holds. He also presently serves as a special consultant to the Menninger Foundation, Fort Logan Mental Health Center, Virginia Institute of Pastoral Care, Iona College Graduate Department of Pastoral Counseling, and the Marriage Counseling Program of the Department of Psychiatry of the University of Pennsylvania School of Medicine.[106]

Hiltner's Intellectual Development

Similar to Boisen, Hiltner has been interested in a variety of theoretical and practical issues related to the fields of theology and psychology. As a pastoral student of human nature, he has attempted to keep abreast of developments in related fields and thus has been influenced by a number of streams of thought.

Few men have taken Boisen as seriously as Hiltner who considers his former teacher at Chicago to be "one of the greatest modern pioneers."[107] Of greatest significance to Hiltner has been Boisen's methodological breakthrough, i.e., his theological approach to psychology of religion and study of concrete cases. As will be elaborated in the following chapter, in clarifying, modifying and developing the implications of Boisen's method, Hiltner completed the shift implicit in Boisen's work, the shift from a psychology of religion orientation to that of pastoral theology. His reference to Boisen as a modern pioneer, then, refers largely to the fact that it was Boisen's insights that initiated this shift.[108]

The importance of Boisen's findings and interpretations with regard to the nature of functional mental illness also has been recognized by Hiltner.[109] However, Hiltner's assimilation of Boisen's views always entails a silent or indirect criticism of the latter's tendency to counter one extreme position by approaching the other extreme. In Hiltner, whose orientation to dynamic psychology is primarily neo-Freudian, Boisen's position is always presented within a broader context or together with other pertinent findings and/or interpretations. In this sense, Hiltner's own work serves as a critique of as well as tribute to Boisen's approach and findings.

The psychoanalytic movement has provided Hiltner with a basic dynamic approach to and understanding of personality. Though he is aware of the fact that there are problems involved in the use of the term "unconscious," he has been less interested in the problem of semantics than in the dynamic intrapsychic forces that influence human behavior and of which man is unaware. Such a view, he states, is widely accepted.[110] It is, in short, an indispensable key which, in unlocking the door to the unconscious-conscious nature of psychological development, has forever sealed the fate of all static views of personality.

In contrast to Boisen's emphasis on what he found lacking in Freudian psychology, Hiltner has consistently maintained that Freud's contributions are too significant to be lost in criticism. While he himself has been critical of Freud's assumptions underlying the orthodox psychoanalytic understanding of religion, he has stressed the fact that Freud took religion seriously, and in so doing, provided the important service of identifying unhealthy, idolatrous forms of religion.[111] Hiltner has emphasized, furthermore, the theological implications of Freud's major findings apart from the philosophical context in which they are presented.[112] Such findings, he has asserted, are essential grist for every constructive theological mill of relevance to modern man.[113]

Freud's dynamic psychology has been viewed by Hiltner as presenting one highly illuminating perspective on the developmental processes and functioning of man. More modern biological perspectives have provided the basis for moving beyond the mechanistic aspects of Freud's position.[114] The emphasis on wholeness of the Gestalt school, but especially as understood biologically in terms of the functional differentiations and unity of the human organism, has informed Hiltner's view of the nature of the healing process.[115] With regard to the basic biological pattern of the developmental process, he has found the theoretical biologist Ludwig von Bertalanffy instructive.[116] The considerable influence of Kurt Goldstein, a neurologist and theoretical biologist, has often been overlooked.[117] As well as clarifying the modern biological grounds for viewing mind and body as abstractions from the total organism, Goldstein directed Hiltner's attention to the significance of distinguishing disease from health on the basis of form rather than content.[118] This differentiation together with Goldstein's understanding of the meaning of functional wholeness[119] threw light on several basic issues for Hiltner. It should also be noted that Hiltner appears to have borrowed the term "impairment" from Goldstein,[120] though he uses it in a more inclusive way than the latter.

As the way in which Hiltner has appropriated both Boisen and Freud suggests, he has promoted and been deeply influenced by the dialogue between dynamic psychology and theology. Those in both fields who have contributed most to his thinking have been those who, as Boisen and Freud, have focused on therapeutic concerns or relevant theoretical issues or both. A number of such contributors, including Harry Bone, Maria Brick, Erich Fromm, Karen Horney, Gotthard Booth, Rollo May, David Roberts, Paul Tillich and Daniel Day Williams, have all been associated in one way or another with the Columbia University and Union Theological Seminary colloquies and seminars on religion and health.[121] Those outside this orbit would include Karl Menninger, Carl Jung, Adolf Meyer, Harry S. Sullivan, Franz Alexander and Carl Rogers in psychology and Arthur Cushman McGiffert, Jr., Edwin Aubrey and Albert Outler in theology.

Among the therapists listed above, Rogers, Bone, Horney and Fromm appear to have been the strongest influences on Hiltner. Ever since he became aware of the work of Rogers in 1943, Hiltner has found Rogers's analysis of the therapeutic process, and in particular his emphasis on the growth forces within man, of theoretical as well as practical significance.[122] Bone, with whom Hiltner taught a counseling course at Union for five years (1945-50), aided his colleague with the task of integrating the case history method developed by Boisen with the verbatim procedure employed by

Russell Dicks. He also contributed to Hiltner's understanding of the differences between the neurotic and "normal" personality.[123] Bone claimed that his own experience supported Horney's interpretation of neurotic behavior.[124]

Hiltner has been deeply impressed with and influenced by the neo-Freudian perspective of Horney and Fromm. Their psychodynamic approach to man's social nature and the human situation in general has helped shape Hiltner's own interpretation of the creative and destructive processes in man. Hiltner has expressed regret over the fact that Horney was less inclined than Fromm to develop the wider constructive implications of her perspective.[125] However, he has emphasized the fact that both have contributed significantly to the further development of psychoanalytic thought. This alone, in Hiltner's assessment, is of major importance for pastoral psychology.[126] That Fromm has been willing to go further in considering theoretical issues of mutual concern to both groups has been viewed by Hiltner as supportive of his own approach. Speaking of Fromm, he states: "In all his thought, psychological, social and ethical, it is clear that Fromm is steadily wrestling with issues that Christianity has always regarded as basic."[127]

Among the theologians listed above, McGiffert, Roberts and Tillich are the contributors to whom Hiltner is most indebted. McGiffert, who taught theology--including a course that he taught jointly with Boisen--at Chicago Theological Seminary at the time Hiltner was a graduate student at Chicago, was apparently the first systematic theologian to attract Hiltner. McGiffert's rejection of all authoritarian approaches to theological method and his employment of various theological methods[128] contributed to the way Hiltner later schematized the various branches of theology. Both in his concern for empirical examination of Christian experience and in his view of theological doctrines as "definitions of attitude," McGiffert directed attention to the underlying processes as the central concern of both psychology and theology.[129]

Another theologian whose work attracted Hiltner was Tillich's younger colleague at Union, David Roberts. Since Hiltner was among those who considered Roberts an astute theologian of exceptional promise, he experienced the unexpected 1955 death of Roberts as a tragic blow. He viewed Roberts's work as complementary to Tillich's and, in some respects, as moving in the same direction as his own.[130] Especially in Roberts's criticism of Tillich[131] and his emphasis on the study of concrete human processes,[132] Roberts had addressed himself to issues which were of primary concern to Hiltner. As has been acknowledged by Hiltner, Roberts's understanding of the dynamic nature of the healing process has contributed to Hiltner's model.[133]

Hiltner has been engaged in creative dialogue with

Paul Tillich more than with any other systematic theologian.[134] He has profited from Tillich's criticism as well as from his own clarification of the differences between them. In his earlier publications Hiltner employed Tillich's categories uncritically. As he developed his own theological method, he shifted to a more critical posture.[135] His deep appreciation of and indebtedness to Tillich, however, have always been acknowledged.

In an article entitled, "The Relation of Religion and Health," Tillich, referring to a passage in Hiltner's RELIGION AND HEALTH, was critical of the latter's failure to distinguish between the biblical and modern concepts of salvation and health,[136] a criticism Hiltner has taken seriously.[137] In his article, Tillich elucidated the cosmic context of the biblical concepts, the essential principles of which he later attempted to present to modern minds in ontological terms. While Hiltner agrees with Tillich's position regarding the primacy of the theological context, he rejects the essential role assigned to philosophy (ontology) in Tillich's method. It is not Tillich's intention --or what Tillich attempted to accomplish through his employment of ontological categories--that Hiltner finds unacceptable. What he cannot accept is what he perceives to be the subtle distortion of man that results when the concrete findings of various disciplines are first organized by philosophical categories in order to render them serviceable to theology.[138]

Hiltner's methodological disagreement with Tillich underlies his dissatisfaction with Tillich's understanding of the relationship of psychology to theology and differentiation between preliminary and ultimate concerns. The former disagreement will be discussed further at a later point in this study. Suffice it at present to point out that Hiltner has viewed Tillich's position as stopping short of recognizing the full potential of pastoral psychology for theology.[139] With regard to Tillich's categories of preliminary and ultimate concerns, Hiltner has been critical of the fact that they tend to be misleading in their oversimplification of concrete reality. According to Hiltner, this type of "gimmick" can be helpful only when approached with extreme caution.[140]

In Hiltner's view, Tillich has been an important contributor to pastoral psychology and theology, but in order to make its own unique contribution pastoral theology must move beyond Tillich's method to a thoroughly process-oriented perspective.[141] Tillich's theology, in other words, fulfills an important function for Hiltner and, in the latter's view, for pastoral theology. Both in its attempt to take human need and the cultural situation seriously and in its recognition of the important practical consequences of theological method, Tillich's theology has provided important clues as well as a strong stimulus for the constructive task of practical theology. It does not accomplish what Hiltner considers to be the major task of pastoral theology.

The primary philosophical position consistent with the nature of pastoral theology, as conceived by Hiltner, is process philosophy. While Hiltner has considered himself as basically Whiteheadian,[142] his interest in process philosophy has always been a secondary matter. He did not arrive at process thinking through the medium of philosophy, but rather as a pastoral theological student of man's total development, functioning and responsiveness. Thus the developmental process theme of unity-differentiation-unity, which is fundamental to Hiltner's view of processes at various levels, is derived primarily from psychology of religion, psychoanalytic thought and modern biology, all of which have informed his clinical theological perspective, rather than from Whitehead's philosophical conceptualization of this theme.[143] Nevertheless, it is clear that Hiltner has found Whitehead's philosophy generally supportive of his own process thinking.[144]

Hiltner has presented two different models, the first focusing on the nature and relation of all forms of healing, and the second focusing more directly on the nature and relation of mental health and salvation. In his PREFACE TO PASTORAL THEOLOGY, following earlier trends in biology and psychology, he employed a form of the field theory model from physics to disclose his understanding of organismic healing.[145] In his more recent discussions of mental health and salvation, he has shifted to the base-value model as clarified by James Lapsley, his former student and present colleague.[146] Both of these models will be considered in this study.

Clinebell's Personal and Professional Development

Youngest of the three men, Clinebell was born in Illinois in 1922. As with Boisen, Clinebell struggled with the impact of painful experiences from an early age. He was only three years old when his younger sister died. This early encounter with death deeply affected him, as did the epileptic condition that began plaguing his older sister a short time later. He describes the latter as "a dark cloud" that hung over his early life.[147]

Prior to the summer before his senior year in high school, Clinebell recalls that he was a shy, self-conscious boy troubled with a deep sense of guilt. However, following a summer camp religious experience which resulted in his decision to enter the ministry, he experienced what he describes as a reorientation of his personality and partial release from the grasp of his conflicts. As a result, he became increasingly involved in extracurricular activities and began to assume leadership roles during his final year in high school, a trend which continued during his college years.[148]

Recognizing that he still had conflicts that resisted resolution, Clinebell later responded positively to the requirement of the William A. White Institute of Psychiatry that he undertake personal therapy as part of his training. While at the White Institute, he spent two years in therapy with a Rogerian-oriented psychologist. Some years later he had further therapy with a Freudian analyst on the West Coast.[149]

Clinebell's parents were both raised on farms in Illinois, and his father, who had studied agriculture at the University of Illinois, continued to be associated with agriculture in one form or another all of his life. Clinebell states that his family experienced the stress and strain of the depression years during which his father struggled to make a living. As a consequence, Clinebell and the other children formed a closer relationship with their mother than with their father.[150]

Clinebell is explicit about the fact that the church and those in his background associated with religion formed a deep influence on his life during his youth. He recalls that the sincere and intense pietism of his grandfather, with whom he spent a number of summer vacations during his early years, made a considerable impression on him. His minister, a man whom he describes as a strong masculine figure who lived his faith, formed an especially meaningful relationship with him. This man became a "second father figure" for Clinebell and apparently influenced his vocational decision. He also considers the support he received from the church in general and the youth fellowship in particular invaluable to him during times of difficulty.[151]

After receiving his B.A. degree cum laude from DePauw University (1944) and his B.D. degree summa cum laude from Garrett Theological Seminary (1947), Clinebell felt the need to seek specialized training in an area in which he had found Garrett and himself deficient, namely, pastoral psychology and counseling. While serving churches during his seminary years, he had become acutely aware of the fact that he was inadequately prepared to help troubled parishioners.[152] Thus upon completion of his seminary training, he enrolled concurrently at the White Institute of Psychiatry, from which he received the Certificate in Applied Psychiatry for the Ministry in 1949, and the Psychology of Religion program at Columbia University, from which he received his Ph.D. degree in 1954. It was during his doctoral program that Clinebell first became involved in clinical pastoral training at Creedmoor and Rockland State Hospitals.[153]

Clinebell also attended the Yale Summer School of Alcohol Studies, a program he later participated in as a faculty member (1957 and 1960). After receiving grants from the National Institute of Mental Health and the American Association of Theological Schools for post-doctoral studies, he spent the academic year 1967-68 at the University of Pennsylvania and Philadelphia Child Guidance Clinic in a concentrated program on marriage and family counseling.[154]

Over a thirteen year period, Clinebell served churches in Indiana, Illinois and New York. While in New York, he was invited to be a lecturer for the Department of Religious Education at New York University (1955-57). After serving briefly in a parish counseling position and hospital chaplaincy, Clinebell joined the faculty of the School of Theology at Claremont (1959) as Professor of Pastoral Counseling and also became Director of the Pasadena Area Pastoral Counseling Center (1959-63). He later served as the Director of the Claremont Area Pastoral Counseling Center (1963-65). At present, as well as continuing in his teaching position at the School of Theology, he is also a member of the faculty of the Claremont Graduate School.[155]

Clinebell's Intellectual Development

If Hiltner is neo-Boisenian and Sullivanian in theological method, Clinebell is somewhat neo-Boisenian and Sullivanian in his interpersonal understanding of religion and mental health. Though as Hiltner he has been profoundly influenced by depth psychology, Clinebell has been critical of those who have neglected the interpersonal nature of mental and spiritual health. In the tradition of such men as Boisen, Paul Johnson and Reuel Howe, he has attempted to move beyond models that overstress either the individual or socialization rather than disclose the significance of both.

From the standpoint of his subsequent development, it is significant that Clinebell's initial studies in depth psychology took place at the White Institute of Psychiatry where he was introduced to the personalities and perspectives of such interpersonalists as Harry S. Sullivan and Frieda Fromm-Reichmann.[156] Sullivan's orientation, the predominant viewpoint at the White Institute, has contributed to the gradual shift within psychiatry anticipated by Boisen, i.e., a shift based on the insights of Mead and Dewey.[157] Thus Clinebell was introduced to depth psychology by a psychiatric school which had been developing a new synthesis with the insights of social psychology. It would appear that by the time he had completed his work at the White Institute, he was already committed in principle to the position he has been expanding and developing ever since, i.e., a multi-dimensional interpersonalism.

Clinebell's graduate work at Columbia exposed him to the views of two men who influenced him profoundly, David Roberts and Paul Tillich. He has acknowledged that it was an article by Roberts on psychiatry and religion that initially attracted him to the (Union)-Columbia program.[158] Roberts, who himself had experienced considerable personal struggle and therapy, viewed the mental health of the individual Christian as a major concern, and under his influence Clinebell moved further toward making mental health one of his own focal interests.[159]

In contrast to Hiltner, Clinebell has embraced Tillich as the pastoral counselor's theologian. Tillich's existential-psychological categories, which attempt to clarify the nature of man's spiritual needs, have provided Clinebell with differentiations that he has considered tailor-made for his multi-dimensional interpersonal model.[160] He has concurred fully with Tillich's view that mental health can only be understood adequately when its theological dimension is taken seriously.

During his Columbia years, Clinebell participated in the same on-going interdepartmental seminar on religion and health that had been so influential on Hiltner during earlier years. As has already been noted, Roberts and Tillich both contributed to this seminar. There Clinebell was introduced to such psychiatric personalities as Fromm and Rollo May,[161] both of whom placed emphasis on the individual's values and the social context of personality development. He also came under the influence of Carney Landis, Columbia Professor of Psychology and Director of Psychological Research at the Neuropsychiatric Hospital.

Landis was a medically trained psychologist who approached his research of psychopathology from the standpoint of both behavior and mental experience. He was also interested in the psychotherapeutic process which he viewed as "properly part and parcel of religion."[162] Clinebell appears to have been attracted by Landis's research interests and understanding of psychotherapy, and he became interested in and eventually adopted a research proposal suggested by Landis[163] several years earlier with regard to alcoholics and group therapy. On the whole, Clinebell profited considerably from the guidance he received from Landis, and the latter became a member of his doctoral committee.[164]

Another man who provided significant guidance to Clinebell during his years at Columbia was Horace Freiss,

Chairman of the Department of Religion and Clinebell's dissertation committee. Freiss was a man of broad interests who had formerly taught in the philosophy department. As a founding member of the seminar on religion and health and editor of the journal (REVIEW OF RELIGION) that published some of the seminar's major papers, he had become increasingly interested in the kinds of questions Clinebell was asking. Under Freiss, Clinebell pursued a program of study which, in its concentration on the relation of philosophy of religion and ethics to depth psychology,[165] contributed to his enlarging interpersonal perspective.

Once Clinebell began to formulate his own position, the strong influence of the dynamic interpersonal viewpoint of Sullivan surfaced. Sullivan had taught Clinebell that the individual (intrapsychic) and hence mental illness and health are abstractions when separated from the social (interpersonal) matrix of the individual's life. By this Sullivan had meant that all of the individual's needs, as a result of the interpersonal way in which they are met or stymied, are inextricably interrelated to the socialization process.[166] To Clinebell, such an orientation was a highly significant modification and to some extent correction of Freud's understanding. Interpreted apart from this perspective, Sullivan's position could be misunderstood as abandoning the individual to the tidal wave of socialization. Interpreted properly as neo-Freudian, it meant that the individual stands secure, but that the most fundamental psychological statement one can make about the individual is that he is relationship-oriented.

Clinebell was convinced that an interpersonal orientation placed the psychodynamic approach in proper perspective, and in doing so, transcended the either/or approach to motivation. It placed emphasis on the fact that motivation consists of a complex interfusion of individual and social factors. Concurring with what he understood to be Sullivan's position, then, he was ready to maintain that the individual must be neither abstracted from nor subordinated to the socialization process. Nor should socialization be viewed as necessarily in opposition to the individual. In brief, both the individual and socialization were to be approached interpersonally from the standpoint of human need and need fulfillment. It followed that mental health could only be adequately understood as an interpersonal process, taking into account the social roots of individual development as well as the individual roots of social development.

Intent upon developing this kind of balanced interpersonal model, Clinebell followed a course similar to that taken by Boisen; he clarified the generic interpersonal-oriented nature and motivation of individual man. Boisen, in accord with his concept of loyalty, had attempted to accomplish this by employing the terms "will-to-serve"--later replaced by "desire for response"--along with Adler's "will-to-power"--later replaced by "desire for recognition"--for describing what he listed as the two major integrative desires of man.[167] Sullivan's genetic approach, on the other hand, had identified the basic interpersonal needs as the "need for tenderness," related to the infant's internal or biological nature, and the "need for security," related to the infant's experience of externally-derived anxiety.[168] Primarily following the insights derived from his own relationship-oriented experiences, and in line with the implications of Sullivan's understanding and Boisen's approach and interpersonal emphasis, Clinebell focused directly and solely on man's gregarious nature by shaping his basic category in the terms "will-to-relate." The will-to-relate, he asserted, is more fundamental than Freud's will-to-pleasure, Adler's will-to-power, or Frankl's will-to-meaning.[169] In short, man's primary need focuses him outward toward those relationships which are essential for mental and spiritual health.

It is important to note that, at this early point in his development, Clinebell viewed mental health from within the psychiatric context of the mental illness-mental health problem. His predominant interest was centered in the depth therapeutic problem of both understanding and helping persons struggling with intrapsychic conflicts. Sullivan was but one of a number of investigators, most therapeutically oriented as Clinebell himself, who contributed to his understanding of this problem--e.g., Freud, Jung, Fromm, Erikson, May, Frankl and Rogers.

During the years that Clinebell was engaged in pastoral counseling in parishes and counseling centers, a gradual shift in perspective took place which culminated in a "broader theoretical base" for pastoral counseling.[170] One significant aspect of this shift was recognition of the importance of viewing mental health apart from the problem of mental illness or intrapsychic conflict. The two men who helped him clarify his expanding position were William Glasser and O. Hobart Mowrer.

Glasser, a psychiatrist who has taught part-time at the University of California in Los Angeles, and Mowrer, Research Professor of Psychology at the University of Illinois, both have emphasized the importance of viewing health from the standpoint of the socialization process. Both have been disillusioned with the psychoanalytic orientation to health and therapy, and both have developed therapeutic models which focus on the importance of responsible, moral behavior. In brief, both men have approached the problems of health and therapy from the standpoint of modern learning theory or a form of behavior modification.[171]

Clinebell's consideration of the positions of Glasser and Mowrer helped him to modify his own stance with regard to the continuity and discontinuity between mental illness and mental health. While approaching the problem of mental health primarily from the psychiatric context, Clinebell had emphasized the intrapsychic continuity between mentally ill and healthy persons. Now he was becoming increasingly aware of the significance of focusing on the discontinuity between mentally ill and healthy persons from the standpoint of the learning capacities of basically healthy persons. As long as intrapsychic struggles or problems were not interfering to any great extent with interpersonal relating, learning and growing could be facilitated in small groups focusing on present experience, including affect, cognition and conation. Since such a shift in perspective placed greater emphasis on the whole-person-in-interpersonal-relationships, it brought out the full potential of Clinebell's multi-dimensional interpersonal model.

Excited about the possibilities of this neo-Wesleyan perspective, Clinebell has directed his full attention to the significance of "the people dynamic" or growth groups.[172] His recent recorded training series on growth counseling, which presents the practical implications of his developing growth orientation for counseling and mental health, indicates the increasing influence of Abraham Maslow and other growth-oriented psychologists on Clinebell's present thinking.[173]

In contrast to Glasser, Clinebell has not abandoned the intrapsychic understanding of health and therapy. Rather he has rejected the assertion that the growth needs of all persons can only be approached profitably from the intrapsychic orientation. The full nature of mental health, in his view, can be understood neither by ignoring nor by reducing everything to intrapsychic dynamics. Thus he appears to view Glasser's position, especially the latter's rejection of the concept of mental illness,[174] as representative of the extreme reaction to the distortions of the psychoanalytic tradition.

Clinebell considers Mowrer's position indicative of what can result when the insights of the intrapsychic understanding of development are not heeded. He has focused his main criticism on what he considers Mowrer's oversimplified view of guilt and tendency to absolutize the individual's value system. In Clinebell's view, Mowrer's failure to differentiate between healthy and unhealthy conscience formation has resulted in his superficial understanding of the relationship of values and different forms of guilt to mental illness and health.[175]

During the course of his development, Clinebell also has been influenced by such contributors to his own field as

Carroll Wise, Wayne Oates, Paul Johnson and Reuel Howe. All four have been interested in the relation of personality development to religion. Wise and Oates, both of whom have been influenced by Boisen, have contributed to the psychodynamic understanding of religion and mental illness and health,[176] while Johnson and Howe have devoted more attention to interpersonal relations and religious community.[177] Both Johnson (CHRISTIAN LOVE, New York: Abingdon-Cokesbury, 1951) and Howe (HERE IS LOVE, Chicago: Judson, 1961) have written books on what Clinebell considers the key interpersonal concept of Christian love. Together with Boisen, these two have contributed significantly to the kind of interpersonal orientation advanced by Clinebell.

In his own attempt to move beyond old perspectives, Clinebell has been attentive to and has drawn support from the views of both Johnson and Oates. Addressing pastoral counselors, Oates summoned this professional community in the early sixties to consider new questions and to recognize its "overdependence. . .upon psychoanalytic presuppositions."[178] From the standpoint of psychology of religion, Johnson has pointed to such research "frontiers" as communication, primary groups, social conflicts and person-to-person encounter,[179] areas which increasingly have captured Clinebell's interest.

Finally, it should be noted that Clinebell's wife Charlotte has been a significant influence on her husband's intellectual and professional development. Her professional training has included such areas as play therapy and marriage and family counseling. She recently (1975) completed her doctoral program in philosophy of education at Claremont Graduate School. The two Clinebells have contributed to one another's perspective on the nature of growth facilitation through their collaborative studies, especially THE INTIMATE MARRIAGE (New York: Harper and Row, 1970) and CRISIS AND GROWTH: HELPING YOUR TROUBLED CHILD (Philadelphia: Fortress, 1971), and their work as co-facilitators of marriage enrichment workshops.[180]

CHAPTER II

APPROACHING THE PROBLEM OF MENTAL-SPIRITUAL HEALTH MODELS

The task of this chapter is to disclose the intentions, assumptions and related problems and issues entailed in the way Boisen, Hiltner and Clinebell have approached their mental health-salvation models. The first section of this chapter will focus on the intentions of the investigators. The second section will attempt to clarify, from the standpoint of Fawcett's categories, the investigators' basic assumptions and the major methodological problems and issues emerging from the analysis.

Intentions of the Investigators

The methodological intentions of Boisen, Hiltner and Clinebell will be considered from the standpoint of their interdisciplinary posture, their theoretical and practical objectives, and the general scope of their pertinent studies.

Interdisciplinary Posture

As is evident from the background material presented in Chapter I, all three investigators have been influenced by a number of theoretical and practical fields. While each received theological training and was ordained into the ministry of a mainline Protestant denomination, each sought further training to become an interdisciplinary specialist in the field of religion and mental health. Each has been a student of psychiatry, and each has functioned as a pastoral counselor, Clinical Pastoral Education Supervisor, researcher and educator. However, the significant differences in their training and way of viewing their specialist roles are of primary importance for understanding their different methodological intentions.

Boisen. Within the context of his role as chaplain (including pastoral counselor) to mentally ill persons, Boisen viewed himself as a clinical researcher and specialist in psychology of religion, sociology of religion and psychopatholoy.[1] His initial study of the causative factors of schizophrenia resulted in statistical support of his view that the clinical facts justify a socio-psychological approach to this serious type of mental illness.[2] Personality dynamics, and thus religious experience and mental health, he maintained, can only be understood from the standpoint of a dynamic social psychology which is interested in the broadest possible context of human development. Nothing short of the total humanization process or what it means to become a full human being is to be deemed adequate. Furthermore, such an interdisciplinary approach, Boisen claimed, is of fundamental significance for the development of what he considered to be the theology of the future, empirical theology.

Boisen's interdisciplinary posture, then, could be characterized as that of a social psychologist of religion and clinical theological investigator. In his view, dynamic social psychology provided the theoretical orientation supported by the facts, and thus it was this orientation from which he approached his research into the nature of functional mental illness, mental health and related theological questions.

Hiltner has come to view himself as a theologian specializing in pastoral theology. While he has followed Boisen in placing emphasis on seeking differentiated theological knowledge, his own theological method and particular career-long interest in the relation of theology to psychology, psychiatry and medicine have directed his attention to a different set of questions with regard to health. In contrast to both Boisen and Clinebell, Hiltner has approached both of his models from the standpoint of total health (inclusive of mental health). As noted earlier, theoretical biology has informed his holistic, organismic orientation to health, and psychoanalytic thought has informed his differentiated intrapsychic orientation to mental and spiritual health. While social psychology has contributed to his understanding of total health, the shape of his field theory model, as will be made clear subsequently, particularly attests to the fact that his primary focus has been the health and salvation of the individual organism.

Clinebell. Both Boisen and Hiltner have emphasized the importance of doing theology, and their interdisciplinary orientations have contributed to the respective ways in which they have understood that task. It is from within the context of doing theology that their models purportedly have been developed. Clinebell, on the other hand, has not been interested in doing theology as such. Though he has been no less interested in pastoral theology than Boisen and Hiltner have been in the practical concerns of pastoral care and counseling, he has approached both pastoral psychology and theology from the standpoint of the modern pastoral practitioner. He has focused his attention on those issues entailed in mediating, facilitating and actualizing sound psychosocial and theological principles. Thus he has understood the function of the pastoral theologian in terms of doing pastoral counseling, not doing theology.[3]

Clinebell has developed his interdisciplinary role primarily from the perspective of the interpersonal pastoral counselor-psychologist with increased emphasis on the function of facilitating growth in the lives of basically mentally healthy persons. He has attempted to bring together and interpret those relevant contributions of religion and theology in synthesis with those of other health related professions and disciplines. His multi-dimensional interpersonal approach to mental health and salvation can only be understood from this orientation.

Objectives

Boisen. As Boisen has made explicit in his autobiography and elsewhere, his general hypothesis took shape during the recovery period of his first hospitalization as he struggled to understand what had happened to him. The experiencer of the mystical phenomena entailed in the outset of Boisen's major acute psychotic episode did not have to search long for a theoretical interpretation which would shed light on his problem. The relevant ideas found earlier in James as well as such authors as Delacroix and Starbuck had been incubating for some time. There can be little doubt that these ideas contributed to Boisen's initial conviction "'that there is no line of separation between valid religious experience and ... abnormal mental states...'"[4] As later stated in the form of a general hypothesis (parenthetical material mine)

> ...such experiences (of acute functional mental illness) are to be explained in terms of the disorganization of the inner world consequent upon the upsetting of the foundations upon which the critical judgments are made and that, as such, it is closely related to certain (personality transforming) types of religious experience.[5]

The primary objective of his research was to establish the validity of this hypothesis. More specifically, Boisen intended to empirically demonstrate that both types of disrupting experiences are initiated by personal conflict situations, entail an intense sense of personal failure in relation to one's loyalties, and are desperate attempts to resolve the conflict through personality reorganization.[6] Boisen's other objectives are related to the way he approached and the significance he attached to this primary objective.

Boisen's related objectives pertained to an historical fact he found disheartening, namely, the increasing division between the field of theology and the fields of medicine and psychiatry. On the one hand, he was troubled by the tendency of the new authority to avoid fundamental value-oriented issues pertinent to individual and social development. On the other hand, he was disturbed by the fact that systematic theology, methodologically content with remaining an abstract discipline, was seemingly willing to abdicate its historical role in this area. In Boisen's view, for theology to relinquish its claim that it has a fundamental contribution to make to the problem of mental illness and health would have dire consequences for both religion and society in general.

With regard to the former concern, Boisen held the general objective of challenging the adequacy of any interpretation of mental illness and health which did not take religion seriously, and the more specific objective of countering the interpretations of Freud. He himself had experienced the results of the failure of medicine and psychiatry to take into account the entire life situation of persons hospitalized in a mental institution. Even when a patient's social situation was considered, the patient's religious experience and beliefs were usually overlooked, partially or totally ignored, or treated as deleterious to personality development. He was convinced that the role of religion in illness and health was not understood adequately and would not be understood adequately until it had been studied thoroughly by a sympathetic investigator.

Because Freud had studied and reached negative conclusions with regard to the way religion functions individually and socially, Boisen approached his research with the intention of negating Freud's conclusions. As Freud, he too was interested in studying the function of religion in mental illness. However, in contrast to Freud, whom Boisen viewed as approaching social psychology from a psychobiological orientation, Boisen was prepared to approach the problem from a non-reductionistic social psychology. In other words, rather than reduce problems of social psychology to psychobiological problems, Boisen was prepared to approach them functionally and dynamically on their own terms. He would then consider the implications of his findings for a wider view of psychobiological functions than that afforded by Freud's method.[7]

With regard to the latter concern, that of theological methodology, Boisen was intent upon demonstrating the significance of a radical shift in theological method. Again he was prepared to take seriously the relevant inference of James with regard to theological method. Boisen's objective was to develop a concrete, empirical theology. This was to be accomplished by asking theological questions of and gleaning theological answers from his socio-psychological conclusions. The task of such a theology would be to disclose testable principles of spiritual life. In short, Boisen's radical methodological shift was designed to develop a theology meaningful to the scientific age. It was, in Boisen's view, the one route available for revitalizing theology and thereby restoring theology to her proper role as "Queen of the Sciences."[8]

Practically, Boisen was convinced that if the religious nature of the humanization process, under conditions of both functional mental illness and mental health, were more adequately understood, better interdisciplinary approaches to both the prevention and treatment of socio-psychological problems and pathology might eventually become a reality. He maintained the hope that other professional groups would recognize the significance of his thesis and be less closed to and even devote more attention to the religious experience of the persons with whom they worked.

In considering the practical implications of his work, however, Boisen pursued the more modest objective of helping his own professional group become more adequately prepared to minister to the mental health needs of parishioners. Christian religion, he believed, has a central role to fulfill in fostering the wholeness of persons. To awaken clergymen and the churches to the nature of this role was of utmost importance to Boisen.[9]

<u>Hiltner</u>. Recognizing the implicit shift within Boisen's position from an academic psychology of religion emphasis to an emphasis on the study of problems more directly pertinent to pastoral concerns, Hiltner has attempted to complete this shift. His primary objective has been to develop an operational pastoral theology as one contributing branch of general theology. This differs from Boisen's objectives in two basic ways. First, while Hiltner has followed Boisen's general method of asking theological questions of concrete process-oriented data, the actual data in which Hiltner has professed to be interested is purportedly provided by the study of pastoral operations or functions,[10] rather than by the study of a group of persons with similar psychopathological experiences. Second, in line with Boisen's intention for his empirical theology, Hiltner has insisted that pastoral theology is not to be understood as merely a practical wing of theology. As well as being of practical significance, it also has a theoretical contribution to make. However, unlike Boisen, he has argued that pastoral theology is to be understood as one branch of theology. He has consistently and persistently emphasized the fact that he views pastoral theology as that theological branch which studies pastoral operations from the shepherding perspective and presents its limited, differentiated findings, as do other branches, to the general pool of theological knowledge for criticism and correction.[11] It should be noted that it

is in that chapter (of PREFACE TO PASTORAL THEOLOGY) designed to demonstrate his pastoral theological method with regard to the healing aspect of shepherding that he has presented his field theory model.[12]

Hiltner has been critical of any approach to the problem of mental health and salvation which employes spatial metaphors and/or begins by abstracting personality from the total organism. The former, in Hiltner's view, conveys the archaic healing-by-invasion concept,[13] and thus his objective has been to avoid spatial models. The latter, he has asserted, tends to distort the fact that the organism is a functional unity, and that all forms of healing contribute in their differentiated ways to that unity.[14] In this regard, he has approached his field theory model with the theoretical objective of clarifying the continuity of all differentiated forms of organismic healing, and the concomitant practical objective of helping pastors develop a modern approach to shepherding and thereby contribute more effectively to the central healing process.

Finally, Hiltner's approach to mental health has always embodied the objective of incorporating the major contributions of Freud, on the one hand, and Boisen (and neo-Freudians) on the other. While convinced that Boisen neither fully understood Freud nor the partial nature of his own insights, Hiltner nevertheless has considered Boisen's contribution to merit careful attention. What must be recognized is that his main objective has been to move beyond the theoretical problems and limitations of both Freud and Boisen in developing his own dynamic, process-oriented perspective.

The limitations of Hiltner's field theory model--which will be fully treated in following sections of this analysis--have necessitated major changes in his understanding of the nature and relation of health and salvation. His intention in developing his second model has been to correct the misleading implications of his earlier model.[15]

It is important to note that, in his attempt to accomplish the latter objective, Hiltner has shifted his methodological focus to a consideration of Biblical theology, what he has called a logic-centered branch of theology. Though he does not explicitly state so, it has clearly been Hiltner's intention to employ the corrective critical process he specified in his PREFACE, i.e., to view critically his pastoral theological findings in light of Biblical theology.

<u>Clinebell</u>. While Clinebell has also found Boisen's understanding of personality dynamics less than adequate, he has maintained that the Boisen-Sullivan focus on the relational nature of mental health is of major significance.

He has been critical of models which abstract persons from their total environmental context.[16] His specific theoretical objective has been to develop a model of mental and spiritual health which has the capacity to illuminate the essential and irreducible contributions of religion and theology to a comprehensive understanding of mental health.[17] In this sense his intention has been to move beyond both mental and mental-spiritual health models which fail to consider man's full interpersonal nature.

It would appear that Clinebell's general objective has been to carry out, on the level of pastoral psychology, the Tillichian program of opening up dialogue between religion and culture. His model embodies Tillich's correlation method in terms of man's need to relate and those interpersonal relationships which answer this need.

Clinebell's main practical objective, coinciding with that of Boisen, has been to involve Christian churches in the mental health revolution. He has stressed the fact that it is their revolution and that failure to recognize this fact would be disastrous. In Clinebell's words: "Mental health centers would then become the _de facto_ churches in that they would be doing more to meet the growth and healing needs of persons than the churches."[18] In his view, then, one of the ways in which Christian churches and pastors must interpret their central task, if they are to fulfill their unique and historical mission, is in terms of mental and spiritual health. His model is an attempt to provide such an interpretation.

General Scope of Major Studies

All three investigators have been interested in the problem of understanding mental illness and the healing movement from mental illness to mental health. Boisen, however, has focused his study exclusively on the various aspects of his one specific thesis on that subject, and has approached his thesis with a predominantly apologetic concern on behalf of religion, in particular Christian religion.[19] Hiltner and Clinebell, on the other hand, have treated a number of health-related topics and have been less inclined to assume an apologetic stance on behalf of religion. They have been more interested in assessing the contributions of religion and the sciences with regard to health, and in distinguishing between that which is worth defending in religion and that which is not.

Boisen. Henri Nouwen has commented on the repetitious quality of Boisen's studies.[20] Boisen's central focus, the relation of functional mental illness to the function of religion, appears over and over again and often in the same words throughout his publications. As he himself admitted, his researching of this problem, initiated by his own struggle with mental illness, became his mission in life. There is no doubt that, from the time of his first institutionalization to the day he died, Boisen was thoroughly convinced that the clue to understanding the human experiment, in terms of both individual and group processes, is to be found in the extreme forms of mental breakdown, disintegration and struggle for reintegration.

In RELIGION IN CRISIS AND CUSTOM, sequel to THE EXPLORATION OF THE INNER WORLD in which his model was presented, Boisen continued to approach his work as a theological clinician. Approaching groups as case studies, he interpreted the spontaneous emergence, decline and renewal of their vitality in light of his understanding of the dynamics of crisis situations. He also attempted to answer questions in defense of his method.[21] If Boisen's tendency to make exaggerated claims for his method is somewhat abated, his method and thesis remain unaltered.[22]

Hiltner. From the time of his initial study, RELIGION AND HEALTH, Hiltner has focused his attention on the various issues encompassed by the relation of general health to religion. Though it raised more questions than it satisfactorily answered,[23] his initial study clearly reflected his desire to stimulate dialogue between religion and theology, on the one hand, and psychology, medicine and psychiatry on the other. His own participation in this dialogue falls roughly into three stages: (1) the early pre-PREFACE stage during which his emphasis was placed on promoting a dynamic pastoral psychology; (2) the PREFACE stage during which his emphasis was placed on developing a perspectival, operational methodology for doing pastoral theology; and (3) the present post-PREFACE stage in which Hiltner has been developing as a dynamic pastoral theologian.[24]

In retrospect, it is apparent that Hiltner's second stage served as a transitional period in his movement from pastoral psychologist to pastoral theologian. That stage, during which he developed his first model, is marked by his attempt to clarify his theoretical position and demonstrate his method. His present stage, in which his second model has appeared, is indicative of the fact that Hiltner himself has recognized the preliminary nature of his work during his transitional stage.

Clinebell. While Clinebell, as Boisen, began his work in the field of religion and health with a study of one specific problem area, namely alcoholism, his interest in the nature and relation of religion and mental health has by no means remained limited to this one area. He has focused, from the standpoint of his pastoral counselor-psychologist orientation, on a number of problem areas, including child development, marriage, social change and leadership skills.[25] His gradual shift from a predominant neo-Freudian depth psychology perspective to a predominantly social psychology of growth perspective, as clarified in BASIC TYPES OF PASTORAL COUNSELING, prepared the way for his present emphasis on the relation of religion to interpersonal growth and the development of human potential. Though the basic shape of Clinebell's multidimensional interpersonal model has not changed, his understanding or interpretation of his model has developed gradually in line with his increasingly broadening perspective.

Methodological Assumptions, Problems and Issues

Attention will now be turned to consideration of the basic assumptions and major problems and issues entailed in the intended methodologies of Boisen, Hiltner and Clinebell. The reader is referred to the preliminary discussion of Fawcett's categories presented in the last section of the "Introduction."

Control and Limited-Relevance Categories of Models

Boisen. What was radical about Boisen's method was his intention to pursue what he called "empirical" theological method. As stated earlier, this was the only available avenue of escape, in his view, from the abstract results of traditional theological method. Rather than begin methodologically with God or the God-man relationship as concrete reality, Boisen proposed to begin with empirical studies into the nature of the humanization process, his data being the experiences, perceptions, and behavior of human subjects in periods of acute functional mental illness, mental health and transition from one to the other. It was in this way that Boisen set out to expose the function of religion and what he assumed to be the concrete ground of theological assertions. The hidden presuppositions which permitted him to confidently make such an assumption will be brought out in the section on "Analogical and Descriptive Categories of Models." In the present section, the author will attempt to take Boisen's stated methodological assumptions and intentions at face value in order to disclose their implications.

In terms of Fawcett's categories, Boisen shifted to the scientific control model in order to study the nature and concrete ground of the religious control model itself. It is illuminating to examine closely the methodological procedures entailed in this intended strategy. First, Boisen in effect was bracketing the God-man--i.e., [God-] man--relationship or metaphysical assumption underlying the religious control model. He distinguished between the God-man relationship which he could not study empirically, and man's idea-of-God which he maintained he could study empirically. Second, he was enlarging the scientific control model to include the reality of human subjectivity. In this regard he was following James in interpreting empirical method broadly to include what in modern parlance would be called clinical (in the sense of case study) and phenomenological (in the sense of taking a fresh look at, grasping the meaning of and describing the underlying processes of subjective content) methods. Third, he approached his socio-psychological findings and interpretations of his data with functional theological questions. While he labeled the results "empirical theology," it would appear to be more precise and less confusing to refer to his position as functional or clinical-phenomenological theology.[26]

In following these procedures, Boisen was making a methodological distinction between that which can and that which cannot be demonstrated on clinical and phenomenological grounds to be concrete. He intended to remain within the boundaries of his method and leave the latter or metaphysical question open. In other words, he removed any possibility of unbracketing the God-man relationship as a final methodological step. What this means is that his intended clinical-phenomenological theology, or in particular his mental health-salvation model, serves as a limited-relevance model under the modified control model of science.

Viewed from this standpoint, it becomes clear that Boisen's intended method is confronted with a major predicament. He had shifted to his "empirical" or clinical-phenomenological method in order to restore theology to a position of prominence. As long as he remained within the boundaries of this method, there was a chance that those theological issues he considered vital would be granted a fair hearing among social scientists, various professional groups and educated persons in general. However, to remain within such boundaries is to raise the theological problem of misplaced concreteness--i.e., the concrete reality of the theological ultimate is no longer methodologically primary --and the concomitant issue of the way in which clinical and phenomenological data may and may not make a significant contribution to theological understanding.

Boisen apparently viewed the charge of misplaced concreteness as the logic of philosophical abstractions. Holding the liberal assumption that revelation is not inconsistent with experience and reason, he was confident that a broadly conceived science could disclose the only concrete experiential and pragmatic grounds for faith in the Christian God, thereby restoring integrity to and serving

Christian faith. In short, the vital issue for Boisen was what theological method could arrive at results which would foster a revitalized and enlightened faith. He was convinced that "empirical" method was the answer.

Clearly, Boisen assumed that if he emphasized both the usefulness and the limitations of "empirical" method, his conclusions would underscore the significance of the movement from symbol (idea-of-God) to that reality (God) toward which the symbol is believed to point.[27] To recognize that such a movement requires a leap of faith propelling one beyond the limitations of clinical-phenomenological method is one thing. However, to be confident that the objective, clinical-phenomenological findings and interpretations pertaining to the purported socio-psychological nature of that symbol will remove barriers to faith--i.e., revitalize the religious power of that symbol--is quite another. The latter is an extremely optimistic position which in effect maintains that theology and religion can profit from science's interpretation of what is considered to be the symbol's concrete content. Thus one criterion for evaluating the results of Boisen's intended method must be whether or not such optimism is justified. In a later section of this chapter, the author will attempt to shed some light on the roots of Boisen's optimistic position. At this point, however, the question must be raised as to whether or not his purportedly objective conclusions actually tend to serve the function of removing barriers to faith. Can a clinical-phenomenological theology, ostensibly developed under the control model of science, attain the status of "Queen of the Sciences?" In Chapter IV, the author will argue that Boisen's intended method, when taken seriously, tends to both foster reductionistic conclusions and hinder the leap-of-faith process for modern man, thereby contributing to the demise rather than the revitalization of theology and religion.

Hiltner. Hiltner's shift from Boisen's method to that of pastoral theology purportedly entailed a return to the context provided by the religious control model. While he was in agreement with Boisen's emphasis on concrete processes, Hiltner was not interested in studying the concrete nature of man's idea-of-God. His intention was to begin with the assumption of the God-man relationship on the level of concrete process[28] and study pastoral operations from within that context.[29] It was from this pastoral theological standpoint that he intended to approach his first limited-relevance, health-salvation model.

It is clear that Hiltner fully intended to resolve the problem of context that had plagued Boisen's method. However, he also appears to have created a serious dilemma by unwittingly intending to follow conflicting procedures. It seems that Hiltner was convinced that he could both begin by affirming a pastoral theological context which, as he himself acknowledges, assumes the concreteness of the God-man relationship, and yet proceed by focusing on the isolated human organism in an effort to glean differentiated knowledge.[30] If this understanding of his intentions is correct, then employment of a limited-relevance model of the organism alone would in effect mean that the relational context must either be ignored or bracketed--i.e., [God-] man. In either case, man would then be approached and studied as an abstraction or apart from what had been initially assumed to be concrete.

Thus, on the level of theoretical procedure, the basic problem of Hiltner's method is which control model is to be pursued methodologically, the religious control model as intended, or some form of the scientific control model. As the above analysis indicates, Hiltner is suspected of undermining his intended method. In Chapter IV, the author will argue that Hiltner indeed failed to recognize the implications of his intended theological assumption, thereby magnifying the importance of rather than seriously treating the contextual issue.

Hiltner's second limited-relevance model, his base-value model, is intended to clarify the fact that he views the issue of context to be of primary significance. In his second model, in order to erase all doubts as to his actual position, Hiltner clearly establishes the dominant methodological role of the religious control model by taking Biblical theology, a logic-centered branch, seriously.[31]

It must be kept in mind that Hiltner's intention in presenting his base-value model is to correct his first model. By turning to a logic-centered branch of theology to provide the corrective, however, Hiltner raises the question of whether pastoral theological method alone is incapable of resolving the contextual issue. Must an operation-centered branch of theology rely on the position of a logic-centered branch to establish the dominant role of the religious control model? It is highly unlikely that Hiltner intends to imply such a position, for it would entail abandoning that for which he had argued so forcefully in his PREFACE, namely, that pastoral theology is as independent as any other branch of theology.[32]

Since it appears quite safe to assume that Hiltner has not intended to retreat from his position on pastoral theology, the question must be raised as to why he chose the route he did rather than simply taking the direct approach of correcting his first model from within his pastoral theological perspective. What will be made clear in the following section of this analysis is that Hiltner has been reluctant to confront the full implications of his contextual problem for his pastoral theological method and model.

Clinebell. As Boisen, Clinebell has been interested in the nature and relation of mental health and salvation from a wider context than that provided by the human organism. In contrast to Boisen, however, he has intended to develop his limited-relevance, pastoral psychological model from within the boundaries of the religious control model. It has been Clinebell's intention, as it has Hiltner's, (1) to establish the religious control model as normative for understanding the nature and relation of mental and spiritual health; and (2) to incorporate the pertinent findings of other disciplines into this context.[33] Regarding the limited-relevance nature of his model, Clinebell has been careful to point out that he views his mental health orientation as providing one significant approach among others for understanding religious phenomena.[34]

Convinced that the clinical-phenomenological data of the self properly interpreted would point to the significance of the Christian ultimate, Boisen had intended to bracket the latter or metaphysical issue and begin with the former. As will be brought out later in the analysis, Clinebell, in basic agreement with Hiltner, has viewed the practical therapeutic importance of operationally focusing on the experiences and perceptions of the person in need as itself rooted in the pastoral counselor's faith and concern. Thus he has insisted that, on a theoretical level, the pastoral psychologist must start with and take fully seriously the assumption of the God-man relationship as what is essential concrete process.[35] From this standpoint, his intention has been to develop a model which embodies the intrapersonal-interpersonal implications of the general normative Christian context.[36] His theoretical point, with which the author agrees and to which support will be given in the last chapter of this study, is that the pertinent clinical-phenomenological data, to be seriously considered from the perspective of modern pastoral psychology, must be approached from a normative, culturally informed Christian perspective.

The problem raised by Boisen's and Clinebell's common methodological intention to focus on man's personality rather than on man as total organism has been brought out by Hiltner. As already noted, the latter has pointed out that such an approach entails an abstracting of personality from man's total nature. In effect such an abstraction means that Clinebell is limiting the God-man relationship to the God-personality relationship. Issues pertinent to the relation of mental and spiritual health to somatic health are thereby generally set aside or avoided. Can this form of specialization provide an adequate understanding of mental and spiritual health, or does it tend to be misleading?

In Chapter IV, the author will substantially agree with Hiltner's position regarding the complex integral relationship between psyche and soma, while maintaining that Clinebell's model provides the necessary psychosocial and theological context for understanding the complex nature and relation of mental health and salvation.

Participator and Observer Categories of Models

Boisen. Boisen's own personal experience had taught him the strengths and limitations of both the participator and observer approaches to understanding human processes. It was as a participator in the crisis experience of mental illness, which Boisen viewed as closely related to his personal religious quest, that he received his own first leads. He was keenly aware of the fact that the participator as participator tends to either accept his present or seek out some new meaning-providing context for interpreting his experiences and perceptions. He also recognized, from the standpoint of empirical investigation, that no meaning-providing context could be considered more than personal data. This, of course, was the reason why empirical investigators tended to ignore such data and focus on observable behavior. While Boisen agreed that observation of behavior could provide helpful information, he was convinced from his own experience that the problem of meaning is of fundamental significance for understanding the nature of mental and spiritual health. He thus considered the choice of operational method to be of major importance.

The participator method, on the one hand, provided the raw experiences and perceptions which begged for elucidating interpretations. From the standpoint of participator as participator, meaning is the central concern, but the meaning the participator assigns to his experiences and perceptions may just as well be distorting as elucidating.[37] Thus alone the participator method, while focusing on the significant question of meaning, is locked in subjectivity with no basis for objective measurement or for arriving at general principles. In Boisen's view, it is a significant but partial method. Alone, it is inadequate for the task of disclosing the full nature of mental and spiritual health.

The observer method, on the other hand, was useful for disclosing pertinent objective information. Boisen made use of the observer method to collect data pertaining to patients' behavior, but he was mainly interested in the relation of behavior to ideation.[38] Thus observations of behavior were considered significant from the standpoint of investigating the relation of behavior to internal experience and perception. Alone, the data secured by the observer method could not expose the nature of either internal conflict or mental and spiritual health.

The nature of the therapeutic relationship and process disclosed the operational method Boisen viewed as essential to his research. Within the context of the pastoral therapeutic relationship, it is the task of the conflicted person as participator to share, examine and gain understanding of his past and present experiences, perceptions and behavior in order to transcend barriers to his/her development. It is the task of the pastoral counselor, if he/she is to be an effective therapeutic agent in the relationship, to function neither as a participant nor as an observer, but rather as a participant observer. In brief, the role of the pastoral counselor, in Boisen's view, is to participate in the relationship while maintaining the objectivity of an observer. The very function of participant observation together with the access of the participant observer to the clinical data of a number of persons provided Boisen with an operational method for examining what he considered to be the significant phenomena.[39]

While the participant-observer method was clearly a description of Boisen's therapeutic role with mentally ill persons, it was also more than this. First, by virtue of the fact that Boisen himself had been a mentally ill participator,[40] participant observation had a more fundamental meaning for him. He was intimately familiar with the type of experience and ideation reported by the persons whom he was studying whether or not he was working with them therapeutically.[41] Second, Boisen had learned from his own experience that functioning as an adequate participant observer was as descriptive of the goal for the counselee as it was of the role of the counselor.[42] This convinced him that the general dynamic nature of mental health and salvation was disclosed by the participant-observer process, a process he viewed as socio-psychological in both its roots and inherent goal. Thus, Boisen's primary operational method resulted in what could be generally described as a participant-observer type of model.

Boisen was cognizant of the fact that his operational method did not resolve all problems. The participant observer's vulnerability to various forms of subjective error challenged his contention that his method could result in objective principles. Boisen's access to the observations of other professionals, his use of the reports--over a three year period--of his own special observers, his employment of a uniform interview--following a carefully prepared list of questions--with most of his subjects, and his use of statistical studies all helped to offset this vulnerability.[43] Nevertheless, there was no way to eliminate fully the possibility of being deceived, being presented with an inadequate or partial picture, and/or being subjective in selection or interpretation of relevant phenomena. The latter posed the more serious threat. Since "participant observer" had a double meaning for Boisen, he was doubly vulnerable to the possibility of falling prey to the latter form of subjective error.

Furthermore, Boisen's participant observer method was basically the same method as that employed by Freud and other psychiatrists. In light of Boisen's intention to counter the psychobiologically-oriented conclusions of Freud, the question of selection and/or interpretation of phenomena takes on added significance. Was Boisen actually methodologically pitting his own biases against those of Freud? Was he so thoroughly intent upon countering Freud that he himself became vulnerable to the same charge he had leveled against Freud, namely, that he as Freud allowed his biases to influence his method and close his eyes to the full implications of his findings? The following section will shed further light on this question.

The underlying issue emerging from the discussion is what contribution if any the pastoral participant observer is qualified to make to the understanding of mental and spiritual health. In the final chapter, while agreeing with Boisen's point that the pastoral participant observer does have a significant contribution to make, the author will basically agree with the intended positions of Hiltner and Clinebell with regard to the way clinical and phenomenological data are to be treated.

Hiltner also intended to employ the participant-observer approach operationally, but in his methodology this approach is considered the preliminary step in his operation-centered way of doing pastoral theology. Rather than utilizing the participant-observer approach for studying a specified group of persons as had Boisen, Hiltner was interested in following Boisen's directive to pastors to recognize and make use of the research potential of their pastoral care roles. In Hiltner's understanding, it is the shepherding person who does pastoral theology when he/she reflects theologically upon the shepherding process.[44] Operationally, the shepherding person as participant observer provides the content about which he/she as pastoral theologian theorizes. As Hiltner defines pastoral theology, it

> ...is an operation-focused branch of theology, which begins with theological questions and concludes with theological answers, in the interim examining all acts and operations of pastor and church to the degree that they involve the perspective of Christian shepherding.[45]

It is clear what Hiltner is intent on specifying: "As an inquiry what pastoral theology is systematic about is the actual process by which shepherding...is brought about."[46]

In light of the above stated position, one would expect that Hiltner, in his preliminary attempt to demonstrate his method, would approach such problems as the nature and relation of mental health and salvation from the standpoint of the shepherding process. Furthermore, especially since he limits the discussion primarily to one-to-one operations, one would expect that the shepherding process about which Hiltner intends to make his preliminary theological reflections would refer to, among other things, the shepherd-to-person-in-need relationship. In fact, Hiltner focuses his attention exclusively on organismic functioning, thereby indicating that the shepherd's participant-observer approach, as Hiltner employs it, does not necessitate the same socio-psychological implications for his model that it did for Boisen's model.

The latter is of major consequence, especially since Hiltner as his predecessor has recognized the importance of developing a participant-observer model. In contrast to Boisen, Hiltner has intentionally limited his first model to the participant-observer nature of organismic functioning. Convinced of the importance of focusing on the socio-psychological nature and relation of mental health and salvation, Boisen had assumed that nothing of significance for the concerns of religion and theology could be gleaned from study of the organism as an isolated unit. Hiltner, to the contrary, has assumed that discernment of differentiated knowledge of the participant-observer functioning of the organism, when this knowledge is understood in its holistic context, is the only way to expose the relationship between the concerns of medicine, psychology and religion.

What Hiltner is claiming is that he can both follow his pastoral theological methodology with its focus on the shepherding process and yet shape his conclusions in terms of the participant-observer nature of organismic functioning. Thus the same conflict which is present on the level of control model also appears to be present on the level of operational method. Since Hiltner makes the claim that, by providing answers to such questions as the sense in which salvation is a form of healing, he has begun the task of developing a systematic pastoral theology,[47] the question must be raised as to whether or not the answers to such questions have actually been attained, as intended, by reflecting on pastoral operations. If, as suspected, they have not been so attained, the problem of what operational method Hiltner is actually following must be resolved.

The issue that arises from this discussion of Hiltner's operational method is whether an operation-centered pastoral theology, as defined by Hiltner, can result from inquiry into shepherding when shepherding as healing is approached from the standpoint of the organismic participant observer or in non-interpersonal terms. In Chapter IV, the author will argue that, by confusing "healing" as an organismic process and goal with "healing" as a shepherding process, Hiltner failed to demonstrate his pastoral theological method and to present an adequate pastoral theological health-salvation model.

In approaching his second model, Hiltner has departed from his operation-centered pastoral theological method and his sole focus on organismic functioning. A major shift has taken place. The central focus is now on values as abstractions from differentiated relations and their underlying processes. Emphasis is placed primarily on man's relationship with God and relation to cosmic process and only secondarily on organismic functioning.[48] Thus Hiltner's second model is an abstract form of an enlarged participant-observer model, i.e., one that is no longer limited to the isolated organism. The values are those of the participant observer who is now the person in the God-man relationship as well as the functioning organism.

If it seems strange that Hiltner, who has always emphasized a process orientation, suddenly shifts to an abstract participant-observer model, it is because the reasons underlying his shift are not immediately apparent. By beginning with the Biblical concepts of salvation and health and selecting the modern, non-competitive base-value model, Hiltner has found the means for combining the contextual corrective with the correspondingly modified content of his field theory model. This approach has permitted him to correct his earlier conclusions with regard to the nature of salvation and the health-salvation relation, continue to maintain the significance of his emphasis on the individual organism and, perhaps most important of all, accomplish both in such a way that defense of his initial model as correct "in a preliminary way" might still be attempted. The latter is important because, had Hiltner concluded that his field theory model was fundamentally wrong and decided to deal with the contextual problem directly on a process level, it would have meant employing some form of the spatial model he had rejected. Furthermore, as already suggested, it would have required major alterations in the way he had attempted to demonstrate his pastoral theological method in chapter six of his PREFACE. In short, Hiltner has had much to gain, in terms of both resolving and avoiding problems, in pursuing his indirect corrective approach.

Chapter III will shed further light on whether or not Hiltner's field theory model of all forms of healing is correct in a preliminary sense. In the final chapter, the author will argue that it is difficult to escape the conclusion that Hiltner has been attempting to evade the basic issues entailed in his earlier failure to demonstrate his pastoral theological method. The author will also maintain that it is in the context of Hiltner's defense of his field theory model that his position vis-a-vis Tillich takes on new light. Finally, it will be noted that, though scarred and though still hedging with regard to his field theory model, Hiltner has nevertheless been developing, via the battle, into a capable process-oriented pastoral theologian.

Clinebell. As Boisen, Clinebell has experienced the participant-observer posture from the perspective of the person in need--though his struggle was neurotic rather than psychotic--as well as from the perspective of the pastoral counselor. He also has found the basic intrapersonal-interpersonal understanding of the participant-observer process to be validated by the clinical-phenomenological data.[49] However, in line with Hiltner's intention, Clinebell has insisted that, for the pastoral psychologist and theologian, the task of comprehending the nature and relation of mental and spiritual health must begin with that which is considered essential to and irreducible within the theological context, not with the participant-observer process itself or apart from this context. His resulting participant-observer model is thus an attempt to conceptualize a psycho-socio-theological interpretation of the humanization process.

From this standpoint, it is clear that for Clinebell the basic methodological issue is the nature of the relationship between theological context and operational method. Whereas Boisen, purportedly bracketing the fundamental question of ultimate concreteness, intended to begin with his operational method for the purpose of data gathering and then proceed to his theoretical, theological conclusions or model, Clinebell has intended to begin with the theological assumption of concreteness and emphasize, within this context, a two-way relationship between theoretical model and operational method. The former contributes to the form and context of the latter, and the latter contributes to the content of the former.[50] For Clinebell, then, the operational method of the pastoral clinician is not data-gathering in the same prior-to-model sense that it purportedly was for Boisen.

What this means for Clinebell's operational method becomes clearer when viewed from the standpoint of what, in his view, may and may not be legitimately bracketed by the pastoral counselor-investigator. As implied earlier, Clinebell is asserting that what the pastoral psychologist and theologian may not do methodologically on any level is bracket the general metaphysical assumption of the God-man relationship. Once this is recognized, the pastoral counselor as participant observer may, on the cognitive level, bracket temporarily his/her own or any theological understanding of God--i.e., [God]-man--in order to focus on the clinical-phenomenological realities--i.e., those pertinent to the counselee's relationships to a destructive ultimate.[51] This form of bracketing, when it takes place, is limited to the level of operational method and then is only a temporary procedure. The operational therapeutic goal is, from this standpoint, the movement of the counselee, with the counselor's assistance, toward unbracketing the God side of the God-man relationship in whatever way is meaningful and helpful for him/her.[52]

Clinebell's approach, by emphasizing the fact that the pastoral investigator's operational method entails functioning in a pastoral role, sharpens the issue raised earlier with regard to what the pastoral counselor-investigator may legitimately study or investigate. In light of the operational methods of Boisen and Hiltner, it is clear that this is a fundamental issue, the operational correlate to the issue of theoretical context. In Chapter IV, as noted earlier, the author will substantially concur with Clinebell's and Hiltner's intention to take the pastoral role seriously on both the theoretical and operational methodological levels.

Analogical and Descriptive Categories of Models

Boisen. While it was clearly Boisen's intention to be descriptive, Boisen did not limit the application of the term "descriptive" to objects. As noted earlier, he enlarged the scientific control model to include subjective phenomena. The question this immediately raises is whether Boisen intended to be as descriptive of the process and relational nature of mental health and salvation as possible within the context of an analogical model, or whether he intended to imply that his conclusions were to be construed as contributing to the development of a thoroughly descriptive model. The question, however, presupposes that Boisen recognized the model-constructing nature of his work. In fact, it would appear that that is precisely what Boisen failed to recognize, and he thereby compounded his methodological problems.

Apparently Boisen, in line with the naive and imperialistic view of science in his day, assumed that the sciences deal directly with concrete reality and therefore have no need to employ models of any kind.[53] At first sight, this appears to be a strange normative assumption for a theological investigator to hold. Perhaps that is because the normative taproot supporting this assumption, as it was held by Boisen, is less apparent to the modern mind. Not until Boisen's tacit but clearly religious normative assumption--namely, that there is an essential (universal), positive function of religion[54]--is brought out into the open does it become apparent that his idealistic metaphysics has slipped out of its brackets. From the perspective of Boisen's fundamental idealistic orientation, no models are required because phenomenal reality is one, is directly knowable, and is viewed as derived from and evolving toward Absolute Mind.[55] In spite of his claims to the contrary, then, what Fawcett has differentiated as the religious control model was actually influencing all of Boisen's work.

In Chapter IV, the author will maintain that the normative assumptions operative in Boisen's purportedly "empirical" investigations indicate that he was misusing his descriptive method, no doubt inadvertently, to justify his own normative position. The author will argue that it is only in light of the all-pervasive influence of Boisen's idealistic metaphysics that his imperialistic approach to "empirical" theology, his optimism regarding the results, and his one-sided interpretations or implicit beat-Freud-at-his-own-game approach may be understood.

Hiltner and Clinebell. Concurring with Boisen, both Hiltner and Clinebell have refused to limit the application of "descriptive" to physical phenomena. In contrast to Boisen, however, recognizing the model-constructing nature of their work, they have intended to develop analogical models and to be as descriptive as possible within an analogical context.

In terms of their actual models, however, Hiltner and Clinebell have approached the problem of the nature and relation of mental health and salvation from quite different analogical perspectives. In his first model, Hiltner has relied on the analogical relationship between a magnetic focus and field and all forms of healing of the human organism. In his second model, he has employed the structure of a pyramid to approach the nature and relation of health and salvation from the standpoint of a hierarchy of values. Clinebell, on the other hand, has developed a model consisting of a combination of two analogical structures. The common features of concentric circles and the relationship dimensions of mental health are further differentiated by the commonality between horizontal and vertical lines and the corresponding in-process dimensions of each relationship.[56]

The different ways in which Hiltner and Clinebell have approached their respective analogical models raises the question as to what, in each case, has governed the use of the particular selected or implied analogical form. Here the question is that of the specific criteria employed by these investigators. The fundamental issue is what the essential criteria should be for selecting an appropriate analogical mental health-salvation model from the standpoint of pastoral psychology and/or theology. In Chapter IV, the author will argue that any pastoral model of the nature and relation of mental and spiritual health must draw its criteria for selecting and developing a model from both the control model of religion and the modern differentiated knowledge about man provided by the sciences.

CHAPTER III

SHAPING THE MENTAL-SPIRITUAL HEALTH MODELS

Attention must now be shifted from focusing on methodological intentions and assumptions to focusing on the structure and content of the mental-spiritual health models themselves. From the standpoint of the structure and content of these models, what is disclosed with regard to the nature and relation of mental and spiritual health? What problems and issues surface?

The first section of this chapter will present diagrams of the models together with their elucidation. The second and third sections will explicate respectively each investigator's understanding of the relational nature and each investigator's understanding of the process nature of mental health and salvation, including each investigator's position with regard to the relation of mental and spiritual health.

General Exposition of the Models

Boisen

Boisen's intended spherical model of the nature and relation of mental health and salvation is a personality-in-social-field model--see Figure 1. It is best described as a progressive or constructive socialization-unification model because it focuses on the dynamic interrelations between personality as a developing socio-psychological self and that part of the total social environment with which the individual identifies at any point in his/her life. Boisen's understanding of the dynamic processes entailed in the development of a healthy personality will be treated later in this chapter. Suffice it to state here that the diagram of his model must be interpreted in light of the dynamic, two-way interchange between an active developing personality and active evolving social field.

The inner circle in the diagram of Boisen's model represents an individual's full personality potential. The content varies from individual to individual in accord with the distinctive features of each.[1] The portion enclosed by a dotted arc stands for the actualized, functioning personality or that which, when viewed from within, Boisen refers to as the self.[2] Boisen maintained a distinction between the ideal self and the actual self.

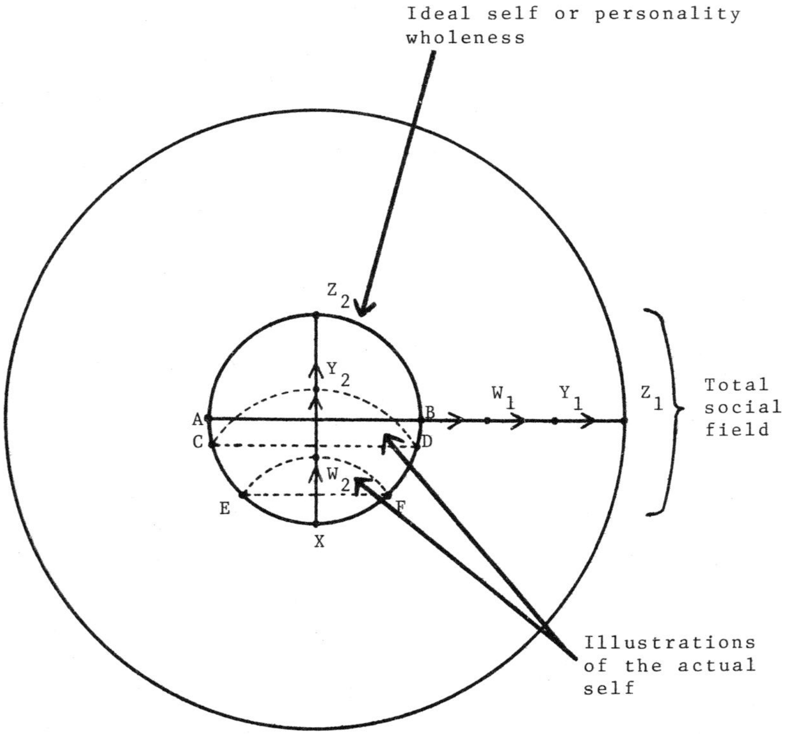

Figure 1. A longitudinal cross-section of Boisen's intended spherical socialization-unification model of the nature and relation of mental health and salvation. Lines AB, CD and EF illustrate the nature of a self's primary loyalty, XZ_2, XY_2 and XW_2 illustrate the nature of a self's ultimate loyalty, and BZ_1, BY_1 and BW_1 illustrate the nature of a self's socialization.[1] The point Z_2 represents the ideal goal of an individual's mental health or salvation, while the arrows pointing toward Z_2 indicate the direction and actual process nature of an individual's mental or spiritual health. Z_1 represents, within the faith stance of the individual and his group, the ideal goal of social salvation for the total social field (mankind). The arrows pointing toward Z_1 indicate the direction and actual process nature of social salvation.

A horizontal line, as illustrated by lines AB, DC and EF, represents an individual's primary loyalty[3] or identification with parents and/or early guides. Where the line is placed in the circle depends on the two factors entailed in the interrelation between the actual parents (and/or guides) and the experiencing-perceiving self. The two determining factors are what the parents, in relating to their child, actually give to him/her in terms of their own lived and/or believed loyalties and values, and what the child as developing personality actually receives and/or how he/she interprets what is being given. The solid line AB, being the diameter of the full circle, represents the maximum start given and/or interpreted as given to the child. BZ_1, the line which traverses the total social field, stands for the highest form of socialization or identification with that group which has the capacity for embracing all mankind. BW_1 and BY_1 stand for less adequate forms of socialization. Theoretically, when AB is equal to BZ_1, the parents have provided a maximum start and the child has received and interpreted it as such.

The vertical lines, illustrated by XZ_2, XY_2 and XW_2, signify an individual's ultimate loyalty or identification with that portion of the total social field which represents the social whole for that person--e.g., XW_2 is equal to BW_1. (Point X thus stands for complete isolation or socio-psychological death, while point Z_2 stands for that ultimate in relation to which man experiences socio-psychological fulfillment.) Boisen distinguishes between the actualized nature of the social group with which one identifies and the socio-psychological ideal toward which one's group points and which the group members, collectively and individually, increasingly attempt to make actual or embody. Theoretically, it follows that when AB is equal to BZ_1, it is also equal to XZ_2. This represents the ideal state in which the child's primary loyalty fully points to that ultimate loyalty in relation to which his/her potential mental or spiritual fulfillment may be actualized.

Mental health and salvation, represented by the arrows in the diagram, are approached from the standpoint of their common socio-psychological nature and relation.

Hiltner

Hiltner's initial model of the nature and relation of all forms of healing is an organismic field theory model--see Figure 2. The total human organism is represented by a simple magnetic field consisting of magnet and files. The magnet and magnetic force represent an individual's personality and person-centered dimensions of processes respectively, and the files represent the various aspects of a person's soma or body.[4] Personality and body are not to be

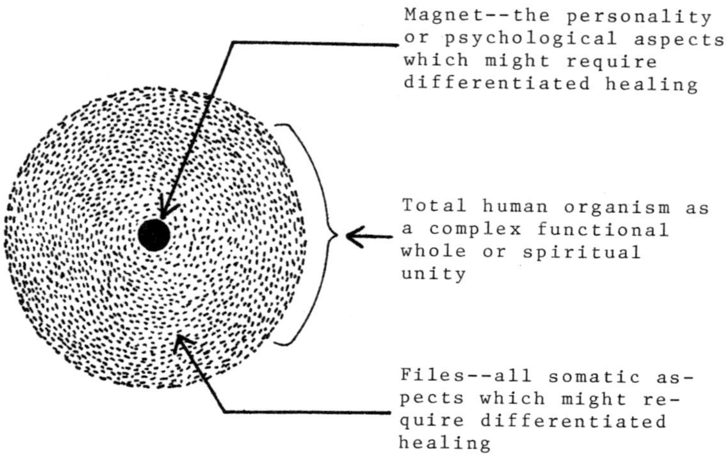

Figure 2. Hiltner's field theory model of the nature and relation of all forms of organismic healing

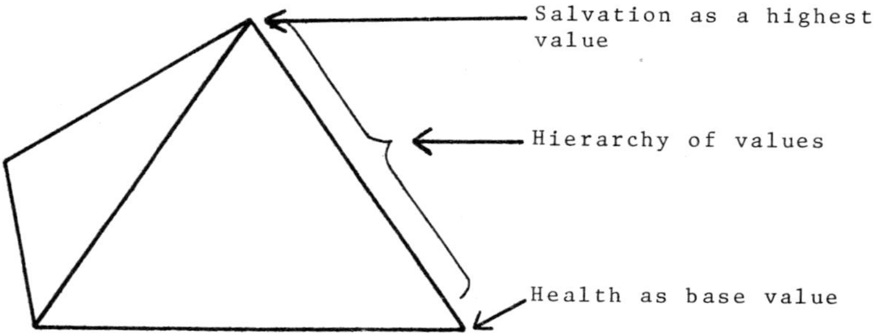

Figure 3. Hiltner's base-value model of the nature and relation of health and salvation

viewed as separate parts but as two perspectives on the total organism.[5]

A model of the total organism is selected by Hiltner in order to consider every possible form of organismic impairment or that which is in need of healing. The human organism is primarily approached from the standpoint of the relation of spiritual healing to other forms of healing. Organized personality is placed at the focus as that which is central to the over-all functioning of the organism as a whole. The degree of magnetic force or pull on the files being a function of the proximity of the files to the magnet, the relative position of any somatic aspect of the organism requiring healing is based on the effect the actual healing has on the whole personality.[6] Thus all forms of healing, from a hangnail to mental and spiritual healing, are treated from the standpoint of the functional wholeness of the organism.

Hiltner's second model focuses on the nature and relation of health and salvation from the standpoint of a hierarchy of constructive values or goals--see Figure 3. A pyramid is employed to represent the highest human values or goals. The base of the pyramid represents the lowest of these values as health, that which enables the walls of the pyramid to be developed. The apex of the pyramid represents the highest of values or the highest goal of salvation. All human values or goals, including love, justice, wisdom, peace and creativity, which are higher than health and lower than salvation, are represented by the walls of the pyramid.[7]

Clinebell

Similar to but more differentiated than Boisen's intended model, Clinebell's spherical model of the nature and relation of mental and spiritual health is a personality-in-cosmic-field model--see Figure 4. It is most adequately described as a multidimensional will-to-relate or community-generating--i.e., will to participate in and contribute to the creation of a salvatory community[8]--model because it places emphasis on the basic relationship-oriented needs of personality and those relationship dimensions and dimensions of relationships fundamental to satisfying those needs. As will become clear in the following sections, it is a psychosocial rather than a socio-psychological model since, in contrast to Boisen's and similar to Hiltner's model, it approaches the self from the standpoint of ego-oriented rather than conscience-oriented integration and identity.

In the diagram of Clinebell's model, the concentric circles of the spherical cross-section represent the relationship dimensions of what Clinebell considers the

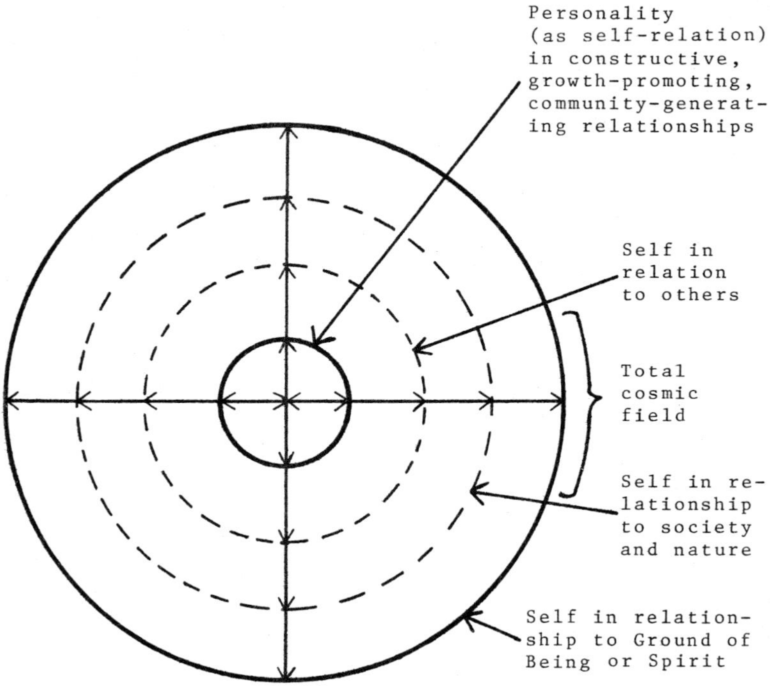

Figure 4. A longitudinal cross-section of Clinebell's spherical, multidimensional will-to-relate or community-generating model of mental-spiritual health, representing the relationship dimensions of positive mental health (psycho-socio-religious concept) with concentric circles, the horizontal (psychological and behavioral) and vertical (spiritual) dimensions of each relationship with the horizontal and vertical lines, and the process nature of mental-spiritual health with arrows

modern, culturally informed, Christian[9] understanding of mental health. The inner circle represents an individual's personality as a self-relation, and each successive concentric circle represents the other side of the self's relationships, that is, with others, society and nature, and God as Ground of Being or Spirit. The solid circumference of the inner circle indicates the unique, separate nature of the individual personality. The dotted circumferences indicate that, in a basically mentally healthy personality, there is a reciprocal relation or continuity present between the interpersonal dimensions. Thus any negative correlation or discontinuity existing between relationships in the life situation of a given individual would indicate some type of conflict, internal and/or external.

The horizontal line represents the psychological and behavioral dimension of the self's relationships, while the vertical line represents the dimension of values, meanings and presence of Spirit in the self's need-satisfying relationships. The arrows, representing the intrapersonal-interpersonal process nature of mental-spiritual health, point to the theoretically distinguishable but practically inseparable dimensions of the process of mental-spiritual health. Finally, the center of the mentally-spiritually healthy personality (and thus of the other relationship dimensions as well) represents an individual's psycho-spiritual relationship with the Ground of Being.

Mental Health and Salvation as Relational Concepts

The structure and content of each model will be treated in this section from the standpoint of the interpretation of the relational nature of mental and spiritual health embodied by each. The analysis of each model will treat those aspects essential to understanding mental health and salvation from the relational perspective. The discussion will begin in each instance with the model's interpretation of the relational nature of man, proceed by considering the corresponding interpretation of the relational nature of mental health and salvation, and conclude by specifying whatever problems and issues surface from the analysis.[10]

Boisen

Both the structure and content of Boisen's model place emphasis on the mentally or spiritually healthy personality as being primarily a social relation--see Figure 1 on page 58. It was not Boisen's intention, thereby to deemphasize the fact that man is a psychological unity, but rather to explicate his conclusion that man's psychological unity is fundamentally social in nature--i.e., the self is best described as socio-psychological. While the whole organism is assumed, the somatic aspects are only considered from the perspective of behavior. Thus Boisen's model, when approached from the standpoint of the relational nature of personality, basically consists of what might be referred to as the internal and external components of the self as a socio-psychological relation.

Prior to explication of the self's internal and external components, it will be helpful to consider the way in which Boisen employs the term "self." Boisen preferred the term "self" to "ego" on theoretical as well as clinical and phenomenological grounds. He viewed "ego" as a Freudian term referring to a specific psychological part-process. Failing to do justice to the social nature of personality, it was a thoroughly inadequate term for representing the nature of the central process of integration. As will become clear in the discussion below and in the following section, Boisen considered the dynamic conscience as the highest evolved emergent and center of personality integration.

What Boisen was attempting to do was move beyond Freud's psychobiological part-process orientation to personality by incorporating the dynamic process nature of psychological development and integration into his Meadian concept of the social self as a phenomenological object of awareness. Thus as Boisen used it, "self" is an inclusive term which combines and views as goal the developing unity of socio-psychological process--i.e., conscience-oriented development and integration--and socio-psychological object --i.e., conscience-oriented identity.

The internal component of the self, according to Boisen, consists of an individual's mental attitudes toward himself and his group. The external component consists of the individual's social behavior or activity which, whether participated in while alone or with one or more others, has reference to one's experienced and perceived social field. Boisen was convinced that the two components must be studied together in order to expose the meaning implicit in both. The same pathological behavior of two persons, he noted, may hold directly opposite meaning for each. The behavior of one may signal a constructive attempt to change self-destructive attitudes and move toward some higher form of self-relation, while the behavior of the other may indicate persistent adherence to self-destructive attitudes and movement toward complete socio-psychological disintegration.[11] The subjective meaning that Boisen considered of major consequence, then, pertains to what the person, internally and externally, is attempting to relate to, i.e., what self-relation(s) one is consciously and/or sub-consciously attempting to choose and enact.

From the relational standpoint, loyalty refers to the

socio-psychological nature of the constructive self-relation. Boisen maintained that the dynamics of integration and disintegration could not be understood apart from the loyalty relation. The only integrative attitudes and modes of behavior, he concluded from his study of mentally ill patients, are those related to the social desires for positive response and recognition.[12] At the core of integration, by which Boisen meant a developing organization of consistent mental attitudes and concomitant behavior, is some basic loyalty to that group from which one seeks acceptance and recognition. Disintegration entails a regressive, self-destructive relation because it is basically socio-psychological withdrawal from the internal and external implications of loyalty, i.e., self and social isolation. Thus Boisen refers to the integrated self as the social self or "deeper self," and contrasts it with what he calls the "baser" self or anti-social regressive relation to psycho-biological drives.[13] Some form of compromise self-relation results when elements of the baser self and social self remain in active conflict.

It is clear that any attempt to choose and actualize an integrative self-relation, according to Boisen's findings, necessitates a social reference group. The important question is what ultimate is conceived by one to claim one's total loyalty. Boisen's point is that this is equivalent to asking about the nature of the actual social reference group which is attempting to actualize and/or the ideal social group which represents the embodiment of any particular ultimate pressing for total loyalty. It is this important socio-psychological fact which requires symbolic expression in one form or another, and the usual form is the personalized idea-of-God.[14]

The idea-of-God, Boisen's clinical-phenomenological findings indicate, is a spontaneous and highly significant aspect of individual and social life. It is an integrative idea personally and socially. On the one hand, it represents the individual's ultimate loyalty and deeper self, that which the individual considers universal and enduring.[15] On the other hand, standing as it does for man's basic need for love from and solidarity with his fellowmen, it represents the collective or "composite impress of those with whom ... (one) seeks identification."[16] Thus the idea-of-God has developmental and/or therapeutic value, and Boisen concludes: "...right relationship with that which is represented by the idea of God is essential to mental or spiritual health."[17]

In Boisen's model, as the structure and content clearly indicate, ultimate loyalty characterizes the fundamental nature of the constructive self-relation. The socio-psychological nature of mental or spiritual health requires not only that there be internal unity as well as congruence between the internal and external components of the self-relation, but also that an adequate ultimate loyalty form the essential self-relation. An adequate ultimate loyalty, in Boisen's view, is individually and socially progressive. Its ultimate significance is judged by the extent to which it has the capacity to foster both self-fulfillment and universal social fulfillment. From the standpoint of these criteria, Boisen asserts, the idea-of-God which symbolizes the most adequate ultimate is "Love."[18]

Boisen noted that sin, which he understood as the rupturing of one's relationship with that which is represented by one's idea-of-God, is differentiated into two extreme forms related to the internal and external components of the self-relation.[19] The extreme internal-external form is the refusal to pursue a constructive resolution to one's inner value conflict between the baser and social selves. As such, it is a conflict which either may be stabilized and thus perpetuated or may be resolved in favor of the baser self, that is, in terms of regressive movement toward disintegration. The extreme internal-external form of sin, in other words, is the refusal, often complicated by long term patterns of reinforcement, to claim any centering loyalty.[20]

The extreme external-internal form of sin, on the other hand, is an attempt to resolve inner conflict in the opposite direction from psychotic withdrawal but via a destructive form of socialization. A centering loyalty is claimed, but it is a delimiting loyalty which, from the standpoint of society as a whole, is anti-social. To the extent that socialization is effected, the threat of mental illness is abated. The price is nevertheless high. As with the extreme internal-external form of sin, the extreme external-internal form prevents the development of that self-relation which progressively leads to the spiritual health of individuals and society.[21]

In Boisen's view, the two extreme forms of sinners, by rejecting a commitment to pursue development of a constructive self-relation, have rejected religion. Their basic problem is that they are attempting, wittingly or unwittingly, to escape religion and spiritual health by avoiding that which is essential to both, identification with an adequate ultimate. In a sense, they have committed the unforgivable sin by consciously or subconsciously rejecting that progressive self-relation which is necessary for mental or spiritual health.

There are many less extreme forms of devious mental attitudes and behavior which, while they may not be in control of the personality, still inhibit development of a constructive self-relation. The significant question, according to Boisen's clinical findings, is the direction in which the person is moving, a question that will be treated in the following section.

The structure and content of Boisen's model equate the

relational nature of mental health with that of salvation. Boisen noted that a person may be a sinner and not mentally ill, as in the case of the criminal, or mentally ill and not a sinner, as in the case of brain injury.[22] What one cannot do is form a non-salvatory constructive mentally healthy self-relation. In Boisen's clinical understanding, the latter is a contradiction in terms.

What Boisen was attempting to do was present a balanced picture of the relational nature of individual and social mental health or salvation. The way he attempted to accomplish this, however, raises a serious problem. As has been noted, conscience is to be interpreted as that evolved emergent which, being inclusive of all aspects of the mentally or spiritually healthy personality, is alone capable of characterizing the individual's self-relation. Yet the structure and content of Boisen's model indicate that his all-inclusive emergent is actually a constructive interpretation of the Freudian superego. As significant as his interpretation is--though itself not without difficulties, as the following section will bring out--the author will maintain in Chapter IV that Boisen's attempt to counter the Freudian position actually resulted in nothing more than requiring the superego portion of the personality to form the self-relation of the whole. In short, the structure and content of Boisen's model are actually far more circumscriptive of the individual than Boisen recognized.

Hiltner

The diagrams of the models of Boisen and Clinebell readily disclose that the relational nature of personality, mental health and salvation is being approached from the standpoint of the relation between intrapersonal and extra-organismic processes. In contrast, the structure and content of Hiltner's first model--see Figure 2 on page 60 --indicate that the relational nature of personality and mental and spiritual health is being limited to the treatment of differentiated, intraorganismic processes in their complex organismic relation--i.e., as they relate to the functional whole. In short, the relational nature of these concepts is only treated organismically in Hiltner's field theory model.

As noted earlier, in his approach to the organism Hiltner emphasizes the fact that by "personality" and "body" he means two perspectives on the organism, not a relationship of parts. Within this context, in contrast to Boisen's understanding of personality development in terms of the relational nature of conscience, Hiltner views personality development in terms of the psychological self or the dynamic differentiated processes of id, ego and superego. He refers to the psychological self as the "characterological matrix," some aspects of which are conscious and some unconscious.[23] Thus he differentiates the conscious self from the total psychological matrix in a traditional Freudian way. While Hiltner does not depart from the Freudian differentiation that the ego functions as the integrating center of personality, in agreement with Boisen, he presents a positive assessment of conscience development.[24] In a neo-Freudian sense, then, optimal personality development is understood in terms of a developing, constructive, integrating relation between the differentiated processes of impulse, reason and conscience. To reiterate, this is viewed as one perspective on the complex unity of the total organism, the nature of which will be explicated in the following section.

Mental health or healing, Hiltner infers, is an abstract concept which is intended to characterize the constructive integration of the differentiated intrapsychic processes. Its significance lies in the differentiated knowledge it refers to, namely, the constructive dynamic relations of id, ego and superego. From the point of view of healing, Hiltner notes, the modern differentiated knowledge pertaining to what is entailed in intrapsychic integration, namely, the assimilation of previously repressed feelings, is of major importance.[25] However, the danger of distortion lies, he maintains, in failing to view this differentiated knowledge from the standpoint of the total organism.

Hiltner's field theory model thus attempts to clarify the fact that mental health or healing is not an inclusive organismic concept, but rather a non-holistic, intrapsychic relational concept abstracted from the organism. His reality-oriented process philosophy has cautioned him to avoid all idealist-oriented excesses. Maintaining his focus on the holistic organismic process and the relation of intra-organismic processes to the functional whole, Hiltner has only employed "self" and "conscious self" in process terms, stressing that it is development or healing of the total functional organism, not the conscious self, that is the object and goal of all intraorganismic processes, psychological and physiological. At the same time, the central role of the conscious self is not deemphasized. It is taken quite seriously as an intraorganismic process.

As will become clear in the following section, spiritual health or healing is approached both as a differentiated intraorganismic process and as a holistic process. From the relational standpoint, Hiltner attempted to maintain that spiritual health is organismic functional wholeness religiously conceived. As with his treatment of mental health, Hiltner was clearly deemphasizing the significance of the full relational nature of spiritual healing or health. On the one hand he stated with reference to functional organismic wholeness:

The nature of that wholeness cannot, it is

believed, be defined in itself but must include reference to the fellowship of the church and the person's connection with it, and to connection with God and Jesus Christ.[26]

On the other hand, he apparently was convinced that if he could distinguish between the mental and spiritual healing processes, the relational context problem would be resolved on the level of organismic process.

What Hiltner is attempting to maintain, then, is that there is a difference between the relational concepts of mental and spiritual healing and that the structure and content of his model are capable of differentiating between them. The question must be raised as to whether or not this is actually the case. As will become clear in the following section and the final chapter, Hiltner himself made an ardent attempt to overcome his methodological problems and distinguish between these concepts, an effort which in the end was unsuccessful. It is the author's intention to substantiate the fact that it was Hiltner's failure to comprehend the magnitude of his contextual problem that prevented him from recognizing that his model is totally ineligible for treating spiritual healing or salvation. The author will conclude in the closing chapter that what Hiltner's model actually explicates is much less than what Hiltner himself has alleged.

In contrast to Hiltner's first model, the structure and content of his second model place emphasis on the relational nature as well as relation of health and salvation--see Figure 3 on page 60. His intention being to differentiate that content from which salvation (as highest value and goal) and health (as base value and supportive goal) are abstracted, Hiltner has selected a model which is not limited to treatment of the isolated organism.

A brief methodological interlude is necessary here, for it was the methodological problem with his first model that led Hiltner to carry out the long overdue task to which Tillich had called his attention years earlier. He contrasted the Biblical assumptions about health and salvation with modern assumptions about health.

It should be noted that it was not long after the appearance of his field theory model that Hiltner, expressing his disillusionment with the term "spiritual health," indicated his increasing awareness of the importance of distinguishing between Biblical and modern assumptions. He began to view "spiritual health" as a term resulting from a confusion of assumptions. It mixes terms--i.e., "spirit" and "health"--which refer to different levels of abstraction, for "spiritual" is meant as a traditional theological term while "health" is meant as a modern term. Thus, in his second model, Hiltner has dropped his use of "spiritual health" as a synonym for salvation.

The structure and content of Hiltner's second model have resulted from his analysis of the Biblical and modern assumptions. From the standpoint of the corrective nature of the structure and content of his second model, it is illuminating to list what Hiltner has identified as the first two modern assumptions followed by what he has identified as the first two and last Biblical assumptions (Hiltner's italics):

> (1) *health is a condition of the individual person;*
> (2) *we use 'health' as referring only analogously to conditions at the social or cosmic levels;*[28]

and

> (1) *Whatever health may be, it is a condition of the individual person only derivatively from cosmic 'wholeness';*
> (2) *Although relatively free functioning (or restoration of functioning) of either soma or psyche or both are seen as positive values, they are not viewed as ends in themselves, as if that context were sufficient;*
> (5) *The highest value is cosmic wholeness (or its restoration), in which the salvatory process enables us to participate both now and hereafter. That highest value is not 'health' in any more limited sense.*[29]

What becomes quite evident is that Hiltner, in developing his field theory model, had continued to confuse modern and Biblical assumptions pertaining to the context of health. While Hiltner points out that the Biblical assumptions are not necessarily opposed to the modern concern with the individual organism, he has given up his attempt to resolve the contextual problem from the standpoint of the isolated organism --his attempt at avoiding the problem in his first model will be treated in the following section.

In Hiltner's base-value model, it is Biblical theology which is viewed as providing the irreducible context and perspective for understanding the relational nature of both salvation and health. The Biblical theological categories of God as Spirit and Creator (of cosmic wholeness) and man as spirit and person[30] (participant, by means of the God-man relationship, in the creation of cosmic wholeness) are considered as primarily and irreducibly concrete. The result is that salvation and health are both understood as abstractions from the fundamentally theological structure of reality which is not provided either by the organism or any collective grouping. Salvation refers to the Spirit (God)-spirit (man) relationship, man's spirit referring to his "true unity and integrity."[31] Man's spirit is thus understood as a different category than psyche and soma. The latter terms refer to aspects of man's organism, while spirit refers to man's true identity as a creature of God. Health of psyche-soma refers to functional wholeness of the organism derived from cosmic wholeness.

Hiltner points out that the Biblical concept of health is not to be confused with "a theory of causation in the scientific sense."[32] He further notes that it is a radically different approach to these phenomena. His point is that the Biblical concern is not about differentiated, empirical knowledge pertaining to healthy organismic functioning; nor is it against such concern when approached from the wider Biblical context. This being the case, Hiltner proceeds to combine the Biblical (theological) and modern (empirical) concerns to form his concept of health as a base value.[33]

Although Hiltner--as will be shown in Chapter IV--fought hard between models to maintain otherwise, the contextual problem of his first model had prevented him from adequately discerning or answering any pastoral theological question pertaining to the health-salvation relation. His second model, by resolving the contextual problem, correctly identifies that pastoral theological question of interest to Hiltner as pertaining to the relation between health as functional wholeness and health and salvation as participation in cosmic wholeness. As will become clear in the following section, from the process standpoint, this shifts the focus away from the isolated organism to whatever dynamic effect man's relationship with God has on organismic healing and vice versa. From the standpoint of the health-salvation relation, Hiltner concluded that this relation is complex,[34] precisely that conclusion which, the author will maintain in the final chapter, his first model had been incapable of conveying.

In the following chapter, the author will note that the structure and content of Hiltner's base-value model provide an adequate way to differentiate between the respective values or goals referred to by the concepts of organismic health and salvation. However, the author will also note that the abstract nature of the model together with the fact that mental health is still thoroughly subsumed under organismic functioning considerably limits its significance. The issue this raises is the theological significance of partial models of man.

Clinebell

As in Boisen's model, the structure and content of Clinebell's model focus on the internal and external dimensions of the self's relatedness--see Figure 4 on page 62. The physical organism is implied and made reference to from the standpoint of behavior. However, as the model's structure and content indicate, the relational concepts of mental and spiritual health are approached solely from a pastoral psychological perspective on the organism. Questions pertaining to the relation of mental and spiritual health to the somatic perspective on the organism, as noted earlier, are not treated.

Similar to Hiltner, Clinebell has approached personality development from a neo-Freudian orientation, including his understanding of the unconscious and personality dynamics. The significance of the unconscious is viewed both in terms of its nature as a "well-spring of creativity (as well as repressed memories and primitive impulses)" and from the standpoint of the buried "roots of behavior."[35] Clinebell views the intrapersonal relationship dimension from the standpoint of ego-oriented integration of the part-processes of id, ego and superego, the latter constructively understood. In line with modern ego psychology, it should also be noted, he has shifted to a position which places greater emphasis on the ego as having autonomy of its own rather than being merely a derivative of the Freudian id.[36] For Clinebell, the individual's personality potential, which is always potential for reality-oriented identity-fostering relationships with others, society, nature and God, is that psycho-socio-religious potential resulting from the ego-oriented integration of the self. From this standpoint, Clinebell emphasizes the development of ego-oriented mental and motor skills and the individual's sense of worth and self-identity.[37]

What Boisen perceived within the context of the nature of conscience development, namely, that there is a two-way relation between an active developing personality and active social field, Clinebell stresses as being of primary significance for understanding the ego-oriented self-relation. In the following section, Clinebell's understanding of the underlying need-fulfilling, relationship-oriented processes will be considered. Here it is important to note that Clinebell, as Boisen, has maintained that the relational nature of mental and spiritual health is as extraorganismic as it is intrapersonal. For Clinebell, however, this means that the self-relation cannot be understood apart from the self's relatedness to total reality. The reality of the ultimate dimension, in other words, cannot be set aside, ignored or denied without distorting the nature of the self-relation.

Clearly creative religion, in Clinebell's view, is integral to personality wholeness because it is centered in the concrete, reality-oriented God-man relationship. From this perspective, sin is fundamentally alienation from God and self[38] and is expressed in all one's relationship dimensions. As will become clear in the following section, Clinebell, in partial agreement with Boisen, also views the dynamic id-superego struggle as often entailed in intrapersonal and interpersonal alienation, but he does not agree with Boisen's simplistic understanding of the id-superego struggle.

Salvation, as the opposite of sin, is reconciliation.[39] As sin refers to broken relationships, spiritual health refers to restored relationships with God and self and the implications of the God-man relationship for the self's other interpersonal relationships. Clinebell prefers "spiritual health" to salvation, apparently because it serves as a kind of bridge concept pointing, in his model, to both the relationship-oriented Source of and the dimensional nature of personality wholeness.

Similar to the non-organismic side of Hiltner's position in his second model, Clinebell also approaches the relational nature of mental health from the standpoint of the self's relatedness to total reality. What this means is that both mental health and salvation, as the model's structure and content indicate, are essentially derived from the self's relationship to God as Ground of Being or Spirit. The God-man relationship is viewed horizontally--i.e., God's immanence--as a dimension of mental health, and the spiritual dimension is viewed vertically--i.e., God's transcendence--as integral to every relationship dimension. Clinebell's model is thus as thoroughly pastoral as it is psychosocial in both structure and content.

What Clinebell is maintaining is that the concepts of mental and spiritual health are theoretically distinguishable but not on the basis of their relational nature. Both are abstractions from the personality in relationship to God, "the center and axis of all other relationships."[40] Mental health is a reductionistic concept apart from the self's relationship to God no less than spiritual health. Nor are these concepts to be distinguished on the basis of value or goal. The highest value or goal is the self's authentic relationship with God from which mental-spiritual wholeness is derived. Rather they are theoretically distinguishable only in dimensional terms. In other words, mental and spiritual health are abstractions from intrapersonal and interpersonal relationship-oriented processes. In this sense, to assert that the mental-spiritual health process itself is essential to self-actualization and growth is simply to affirm, from the relational standpoint, that the God-man relationship is the primary salvatory Ground and goal of the self-relation.

It should be noted, then, that the structure and content of Clinebell's model are spatial only in the sense of attesting to the internal and external reality of all genuine relationships. From the relational standpoint, the model's focus is clearly on the multidimensional, relationship-oriented nature of mental-spiritual health. This being the case, in the final chapter the author will maintain that the structure and content of Clinebell's model effectively convey the relational nature of and relation of mental and spiritual health. However, further structure is needed if the model is to consider the complex issue of the relation of mental and spiritual health to the physical organism, an issue Clinebell has thus far skirted.

Mental Health and Salvation as Processes

In the present section, the structure and content of the four models will be considered from the perspective of the dynamic process nature of mental health and salvation each directly or indirectly attempts to disclose. The exposition will attempt to consider all those aspects of the structure and content of each model pertinent to the nature of the focal processes. Similar to the preceding section, the discussion will begin in most instances with the model's interpretation of the nature of the relevant human processes, proceed by considering the corresponding interpretation of the process nature of mental health and salvation, and conclude by clarifying whatever problems and issues emerge from the analysis.

Boisen

Approached from the standpoint of processes, the structure and content of Boisen's model--see Figure 1 on page 58--identify the primary and secondary processes[41] of personality development with the socio-psychological dynamics of loyalty. The primary process is that of primary loyalty formation or internalization of parental loyalties and values.[42] The secondary process is that of transcending one's primary loyalty and forming one's own ultimate loyalty, i.e., clarifying the nature of and identifying with what one conceives to be an adequate ultimate.[43] To be involved in this process is to be maturing in the participant-observer process, becoming increasingly effective in evaluating and integrating one's experiences and constructively directing one's life course.

The primary process begins during that early stage of life when the infant is totally helpless and dependent on parental care. Boisen implies that the beginning of the primary process is the initial and rudimentary phase of the participant-observer process. At this point the child is an active participant observer only in the sense that he internalizes what he experiences and perceives in relation to his parents and early guides. Since he does not yet have the ability to be critically selective, socialization during this early stage is necessarily a one-way feeding process. That is to say that the infant is a social initiate, a recipient who adopts those loyalties and values which significant others convey are essential for his socio-psychological development. In brief, being the range of his limited experience, the child learns to perceive, value and judge through the eyes of his parental figures.[44]

The secondary process begins when the child starts to raise value questions and make decisions for himself. Prior to this stage, the only ultimate loyalty available to the child is that which is implicit within his/her primary loyalty or internal identification with parents and early guides. In other words, the loyalties and values of significant others, as experienced, perceived and internalized by the child, point beyond themselves to some ultimate loyalty. This is equivalent to saying that the only ultimate loyalty the child knows is that which his parents and early guides represent. Boisen noted that Freudians tended to overlook this important point.[45] Once it is grasped, he maintained, it becomes clear that the main socio-psychological developmental task is transcending one's primary loyalty and clarifying the nature of and identifying with that which is worthy of one's ultimate loyalty.

The secondary process is thus the movement toward independence from parental authority and interdependence with one's group. When this process proceeds positively or without major difficulty, or when it is pursued following a major disruption in the life pattern one has been living, elements of one's primary loyalty are assimilated into one's more comprehensive loyalty.[46] In Boisen's view, this is a lifelong developmental process which, whether or not it entails changing or modifying one's claimed ultimate, includes working out and actualizing the implications of one's ultimate in all areas of one's life. Socially, it entails the goal of attempting to bring about a utopia.[47]

Boisen implies that the secondary process is dependent on the individual's development as an adequate participant observer or experiencer-evaluator, both in the sense of becoming increasingly aware of what is entailed in evaluating and integrating one's experiences, and in the sense of actually doing these effectively. As the structure and content of Boisen's model attempt to indicate, the central issue is whether or not the participant observer recognizes and accepts responsibility for the fact that his individual fulfillment is not only social in nature, but constructively social. Boisen points out that this is true in the general sense that the implicit goal of the participant-observer process is the development of an adequate system of meanings or an affirmative philosophy of life. Such a goal is necessarily social due to the fact that it depends on collective symbols or language. It is constructively or creatively social, whether or not it includes anything functionally novel for mankind, in the sense and to the extent that social value is realized by the individual as he/she actualizes his/her ultimate loyalty. Boisen points out that it is also true in the more basic sense that one must become an active socializer in order to assimilate one's experiences. This, in Boisen's understanding, is the connective socio-psychological dynamic underlying the creative socialization-unification process, and thus it will be helpful to dwell momentarily on what Boisen means by active socializer and assimilator.

What struck Boisen about his own earlier life situation and that of the mentally ill patients and historical persons (during their periods of inner conflict) he studied was the fact that they all could be characterized as reacting in one way or another to a sense of guilt, fear of rejection, isolation and failure. They were not active socializers in the sense that they chose to deceive themselves and others and/or withdraw from their groups rather than risk verbalizing or sharing that which troubled them. All failed to recognize and/or do anything about the fact that they could not assimilate troublesome, guilt-producing experiences which they chose to conceal rather than share. Boisen referred to such unassimilated experiences as analogous to undigested food, both being disruptive of healthy normal functioning. The clinical evidence indicated, Boisen concluded, that the assimilation process is coincidental with the socialization process. One cannot assimilate what one is unwilling to share honestly and openly with one's group.[48]

Socialization and personality unification were thus understood by Boisen as different aspects of the same concrete process. His point is that when socialization and personality unification are viewed, as the facts insist they must be, in light of the progressive, constructive principle embodied in the secondary process, the essential function of religion and concrete nature of mental or spiritual health are exposed.

The evidence provided by Boisen's study of the ideation of his psychotic and historical subjects convinced Boisen that he was justified in associating religion with the striving of persons to become better.[49] The essential function of religion is thus identified with the social and personal effort to actualize ideals.[50] Religion is the attempt to establish and promote the highest form of socialization. From the standpoint of the individual, Boisen states:

> Religion is thus social in origin and it seeks to meet the need for social response and security in the attempt to identify the individual self with that which is felt to be universal and abiding in human society.[51]

From the standpoint of the group, he states:

> Organized religion is thus the attempt to provide for the perpetuation and extension of the profounder insights and the moral achievements of the race and for co-operative pursuit of the better personal and social life on the basis of an accepted ideal toward which we are moving and of its concomitant hierarchy of values.[52]

Boisen was convinced that the meaning underlying such experiences, perceptions and/or behavior as acute anxiety, delusions of being Christ or God, excessive self-blame, etc., and the psychotic--referring to cases in which religious concern was undeniably present--but somewhat socialized personality reconstruction, could only be understood in terms of the essential function of religion. Acute anxiety, according to Boisen, is awareness of some serious threat to self-integrity, and thus it is a call for mobilization of resources in order to overcome the danger and get back on the track of actualizing one's ideal self.[53] Delusions of grandeur and excessive self-blame are to be viewed as striking attempts to resolve the problem of fully identifying with and conforming one's behavior to an adequate ultimate loyalty.[54] With regard to those stabilized psychotics in Boisen's study whose religious concern was intertwined with their delusions, Boisen contended that their benign attitudes were a result of their religious concern, inferring that this too was to be viewed in a positive light.[55] In brief, Boisen was intent upon ruling out the possibility that religion is ever an escape from reality.

While the essential function of religion is identified with the progressive loyalty-oriented nature of the socialization-unification process, mental health and salvation are approached, respectively, as modern and traditional ways of conceptualizing participation in this process. Both refer to the developmental process, whether this entails a depth unburdening of guilt, the gradual educational process of increasingly actualizing one's insights into what is entailed in developing one's full socio-psychological potential, or something in between. In other words, both refer to the direction of the process or movement away from guilt, isolation and disintegration and toward forgiveness, openness and integration.[56]

Boisen implies that mental health and spiritual health may be understood as separate concepts referring to separate processes only when the unity and creative evolutionary function of the socialization-unification process are disregarded. By linking the essential function of religion with the socialization-unification process, Boisen is attempting to maintain that anything less than active participation in this kind of constructive socio-psychological development is less than fulfilling. In Boisen's view, then, any attempt to avoid, escape or renounce involvement in the creative socialization-unification process necessarily results in an unsuccessful attempt at actualizing one's spiritually whole, ideal self. His point is that when the individual (and/or group) actually participates in some life pattern falling outside the parameters of the progressive socialization-unification process, wittingly or unwittingly, he/she (and/or the group) at best has attempted to effect a recessive form of socialization-unification. The inference is that an extreme attempt at enacting separation of mental health from spiritual health or vice versa--e.g., as characterizes what the non-mentally ill criminal is attempting to accomplish, on the one hand, and what the mentally ill person who claims to be Christ is attempting to accomplish, on the other hand--when viewed from the context of the whole conscience, is recognized for what it basically is, an attempt to perpetuate the life of some experimental branch on the socio-psychological tree of life that is doomed to extinction. Furthermore, in Boisen's view, it is this kind of destructive tendency to which "normal" or average man unwittingly contributes, to some degree or other, by failing to claim and live an adequate ultimate.[57]

Boisen was clearly promoting a dynamic view of conscience formation and development that embodied important aspects of what is entailed in actually becoming a whole, integrated person. He recognized that outward conformity is but a compromise solution to life's problems, and that it is the congruence between socialization and unification that is of primary significance. However, perfectionistic elements entered into his dynamic formulation. The task of every man, Boisen asserted, is to strive after "the best" in terms of the deepest need and highest personal and social ideal, that of "Love."[58] From the standpoint of the psycho-theological goal, his vision of whole man was clouded by his emphasis on identifying with ideals, viewing the central problem in either/or id-superego terms--i.e., one or the other becoming master of the psyche--and in his concomitant failure to fully understand the nature of integration. From the standpoint of the socio-theological "Greater-than-self" or ideal of "Love," his vision was clouded by the subtle conditional element implicit within his understanding: "Love ... in whose eyes no one is condemned who is in the process of becoming better."[59]

What Boisen was attempting to maintain is that the

clinical-phenomenological evidence, which both sheds light on and is illuminated by the nature of the struggles and breakthroughs of historical religious figures, rules out the possibility that religion is ever an escape from reality. The key question, of course, is how the clinical-phenomenological material should be interpreted. It becomes increasingly clear that interpreting the data from a socio-psychological perspective meant, for Boisen, interpreting all human phenomena from the standpoint of establishing the superego at the center of personality and society.

From the process standpoint, the structure and content of Boisen's model convey a perfectionistic interpretation of the goal of mental and spiritual health. In the final chapter, the author will conclude that Boisen neither recognized the destructive imbalance in his understanding of personality development nor the reinforcement of this imbalance by his idealistic understanding of religion.

The basic issue this raises is whether or not mental or spiritual health is adequately understood as a process moving toward any form of individual and social perfection. In the following chapter, the author will substantially agree with the position of Hiltner and Clinebell that perfectionistic elements in religion tend to foster problems in personality development. Thus any orientation to pastoral psychology and/or religion that fails to take this into account is inadequate.

Hiltner

The structure of Hiltner's field theory model together with the questions pertaining to the healing process[60] he is asking make explicit the kind of differentiated content he is attempting to emphasize. He is interested in disclosing the forms and continuity of intraorganismic healing, including mental and spiritual healing, from the standpoint of the functionally whole organism--see Figure 2 on page 60. Anything in the organism's environment affecting it is necessarily treated from this intraorganismic perspective.

The healing process is defined by Hiltner as "the restoration of functional wholeness that has been impaired as to direction and/or schedule" (Hiltner's italics).[61] Hiltner points out that the only necessary similarity between the organism prior to its impairment or need of healing and the organism restored or after healing has taken place is the characteristic of functional wholeness. The organism's structural details may change as in the case of an accidental loss of limb, removal of a diseased kidney, a heart transplant, or the correction of some congenital loss or deformity. While some structure clearly is essential, permanent structural loss or change may be present after healing has taken place. Hiltner further asserts that it is not a failure in healing when a loss of function not essential to organismic functional wholeness accompanies structural loss or change. Such a loss, in his view, is properly considered a functional handicap.[62]

By restoration of functional wholeness, Hiltner does not mean a static state but rather the dominant emergence of the healing process which counters the previously dominant impairment process. Restoration of functional wholeness, of course, may not be possible, as when a ravaging cancerous condition becomes irreversible, or it may not be needed. In the case of the latter, the dominant process of the organism is characterized as functionally whole, meaning that at that time nothing is inhibiting to any significant extent the integrating tendencies and integrated functioning of the organism. It is moving, though not in any simplistic developmental unfolding fashion, in the direction of its fulfillment.

Before we turn to a consideration of Hiltner's differentiated causal categories of impairment, it will prove helpful to clarify the way Hiltner defines and understands the developmental process. "Development" is a significant organismic process term for Hiltner, but its full organismic meaning can only be grasped after it has been extricated from its exclusively biological reference. Hiltner points out that while schedule and direction refer to the biological development of structures, functions and processes, they also necessarily refer to personality development in which decision-making plays a significant role. Thus he defines "development" from his whole organism orientation as "that process by which natural organic sequences and personal decision are related (mutually or in tension) in the emergence or production of human beings."[63]

Hiltner emphasizes the complexity of the developmental process of the organism as it moves from one level of unity to differentiations and on to a higher level of integrated unity. The seemingly less important, nondramatic choices and developments as well as the obviously significant critical moments, stages and decisions, the slowing down and the spurting ahead, the enrichening and expanding, all contribute to the organism's development both in terms of schedule and direction.[64]

Because that which disrupts the developmental process is also complex, referring to it objectively as a disease process and subjectively (experientially) as illness, Hiltner argues, is appropriate regardless of whether the specific condition is identified as schizophrenia or a viral infection. As with the term "development," Hiltner attempts to extricate the terms "disease" and "illness" from any exclusivistic usage which would rule out the possible role of decision-making--Hiltner's understanding of the decision-making process will be explicated subsequently. The complexity that he is convinced "disease process" effectively conveys is the relentless, inflexible, dominating nature of serious organismic impairment, the healing of which requires adequate, differentiated knowledge and adequately differentiating decisions. The complexity conveyed by "illness," a term which links the disease process with the subjective experience of same, is the painful and preoccupying reality of the experience which complicates the decision-making process.[65]

All possible factors that could impair the organism and disrupt development are differentiated by Hiltner into four basic causal categories of defect, invasion, distortion and decision. The first three categories are defined in broad terms in order to include psychological and social as well as physical types of defect, invasion and distortion. Thus, according to Hiltner, impairments classed as defects might include to some extent the psychopathic personality as well as the person born without hearing; those classed as invaders might include the overdependent personality resulting from parental invasion (in a symbiotic sense) as well as a bacterial infection; and those classed as distortions might include acceptance of the development-limiting goals of others as well as vitamin deficiency.[66]

The fourth causal category of decision pertains to the exercise of freedom of choice. It is different than the other categories in that, to whatever extent it is a causal factor in any given disease process, it also is a factor in the healing process. While it may play a limited role in some forms of healing, such as that of a hangnail or a bruised arm, it may play an important or even decisive role in others, such as the healing of a common cold, heart condition or hysterical paralysis.[67]

Hiltner states that by decision-making he does not mean to imply a necessarily conscious process or awareness of all the factors influencing the decision. The fact is that the individual is making decisions all the time without necessarily being cognizant of the nature of either his limited freedom of choice or the other factors entailed in the actual choices. As with the juvenile delinquent brought up fatherless in a poverty-stricken neighborhood, the factor of decision may have been greatly limited all along by a number of factors, some conscious some unconscious, which were contributing to his/her antisocial development. Hiltner's point is that the factor of choice, however limited and however difficult to exercise, is always operative to some extent or other. At any point in time, it may be exercised in such a way that it functions either as a causative factor of disease or as a positive healing factor attempting to overcome the dominance of negative factors.[68]

What Hiltner is attempting to clarify is the following: (1) the complex causality of any specific disease process to which factors from several or all four differentiated categories may contribute; (2) the correspondingly complex nature of the healing process which may require differentiated means of organismic healing, including medical, depth psychological and/or pastoral means; and (3) both of the above in light of the complexity of the developmental process which, when free from impairment, moves unsteadily yet positively (from the viewpoint of the whole organism) from one level of unity to differentiations and on toward a higher level of complex unity. It is clear that Hiltner's model attempts to explicate the complexity of psychobiological unity, not in the Freudian mechanistic sense, but rather in terms of the integration of differentiated intraorganismic processes. The individual as decision-maker is viewed as integrally related to other significant factors affecting total development, on the one hand, and impairment and healing on the other. It is in this context that participant-observer nature of the self is of central importance.

The participant observer characterizes the conscious, intraorganismic processes relevant to decision-making, including self-experience, self-recollection, self-input (selecting, evaluating, deciding), and the perceptions or insights pertaining to that experience, remembering and input. Its significance emerges from Hiltner's understanding of the developmental process and is explicated further in his discussion of sin and spiritual healing.

Because of the complex relation between natural organic sequences and decision-making, the organism's developing capacity as an increasingly integrated personality is essential to the movement from unity to differentiations to a higher level of complex unity or organismic integration. Consciousness being paramount to this process, the participant observer plays a central role in whatever integration takes place. It contributes, for better or for worse, to the direction, pace and quality of its own organismic developmental process. If it is to be for better or primarily constructive, then the self as participant observer must adequately carry out its developmental integrating function by discerning and making constructive use of differentiated knowledge about its own psychological matrix and natural organic sequences. Clearly the implication is that the participant observer contributes to the constructive development of the organism by both increasing the organism's awareness of its total nature and by pursuing that kind of holistic integration and those kinds of differentiating decisions which, in their mutual reinforcement, are supportive and enhancing of the organism's functional wholeness.

The organismic processes underlying the general theological concepts of "sin" and "salvation of the soul" (when "soul" means and is replaced by "spirit"[69]) are considered by Hiltner in light of his understanding of the conscious self as participant observer. The basic pastoral theological question is what do sin and salvation mean from the perspective of both the differentiated processes and the holistic process of impairment and healing. On the abstract level of general theology, sin roughly means, according to Hiltner, "man's alienation from God and from his own true fulfillment for which he bears responsibility."[70] On the intraorganismic level, Hiltner points out, sin refers to that differentiated process described as irresponsibility in decision-making. It entails a failure on the part of the participant-observer to identify and/or make a constructive choice with regard to that for which the self is responsible.[71]

When this differentiation is viewed from the standpoint of the complex functional unity of the total organism from which it has been abstracted, its pervasive, centrally impairing nature becomes clear. The participant observer's irresponsibility reinforces and is reinforced by other factors contributing to impairment. This increasingly destructive, determining process makes it more and more difficult for the conscious self to reverse the degenerative process and fulfill a central role in restoring the organism's functional wholeness.[72]

Hiltner implies that on the abstract level of general theology salvation means the opposite of sin or reconciliation with God and self. On the intraorganismic level, salvation or spiritual healing as a differentiated process refers to responsibility in decision-making. It entails success on the part of the participant observer in identifying, taking seriously and making a constructive decision with regard to that for which the conscious self is responsible. Hiltner points out that the decision that needs to be made to be as constructively effective as possible in countering any particular degenerative process, is often that decision which, due to the individual's characterological matrix, is most difficult for his/her conscious self to make and pursue.[73]

From the holistic perspective religiously conceived, according to Hiltner: "What is most important to have healed is man's spirit, his total personality, his sinful (because free) self."[74] The centrally healing nature of responsible decision-making is evident in its liberating effects, enabling the organism, Hiltner attempts to maintain, to make whatever movement toward over-all functional wholeness is possible. Hiltner's point is that salvation refers to that new level of complex functional healing and resulting unity of the organism made psychologically possible, whether or not it is fully attainable,[75] by responsible decision-making.

Due to the preoccupying nature of any type of impairment, Hiltner asserts, one's over-all functional wholeness may be effected. The more serious the impairment, the more likely this is to occur. What Hiltner means is that illness makes it difficult to maintain proper perspective with regard to that which is and is not of central importance to the participant-observer organism. However, just as any impairment may be an inducement to become preoccupied with some aspect of the organism, so any type of differentiated healing may likewise serve as an inducement to reassess that which is of central importance to the functionally whole organism. If the latter does take place, then the healing, regardless of type, has a religious dimension. In Hiltner's words: "It is its effect upon the production of functional wholeness that indicates the degree and kind of its religious dimension and depth" (Hiltner's italics).[76]

What Hiltner is asserting is that the differentiated processes of physical, psychological and spiritual healing, when viewed from the perspective of the highest attainable level of complex organismic integration, are recognized as dimensions of the central healing process. As differentiated processes, they are dominant dimensions of differentiated types of healing. While they, as such, are vitally useful from the standpoint of differentiated knowledge and specialized approaches to healing, failure to recognize them as abstracted dimensions inevitably leads to some distortion in comprehending the complex nature of holistic or over-all healing. Again, as aspects of the latter, they are healing dimensions of the organismic process viewed from the perspective of the whole.

Once the holistic nature of that from which spiritual healing is abstracted is recognized, the centrally important nature of spiritual healing, from the standpoint of religion, makes this concept uniquely suitable for characterizing the inclusive process goal of over-all functional wholeness. Does this not mean, after all, that the religious control model is actually contributing to the content of Hiltner's model?

Hiltner was clearly attempting to maintain that both the organism and religion determine the norm.[77] He recognized that failure to do so would necessarily result in reductionism, i.e., the content of spiritual healing or health would be equated with the content of holistic healing or complex organismic integration, and the latter would be inseparable from mental healing or health holistically conceived. His desire to avoid this at all costs apparently led him to the abstract conclusion that spiritual health was only to be identified with the form of organismic functional wholeness, not its content. In his words: "Such a position, it should be carefully noted, does not make Christian healing or salvation synonymous with ideas such as adjustment, maturity, or any possible content definition of functional wholeness."[78] What is important to note is that it was the contextual problem or choice of model that in the end forced Hiltner to resort to the abstract form-content distinction in a final effort to avoid the charge of reductionism.

It is precisely at this point that the serious problem confronting the structure and content of Hiltner's field theory model becomes apparent. The fundamental question is whether or not the structure and content of the field theory model are capable of embodying the religious norm for what is and is not to be interpreted as salvatory for man. Does the form-content distinction accomplish this? In other words, are the structure and content of Hiltner's model capable of accounting for the kind of discontinuity between the spiritual and other dimensions of holistic healing Hiltner was attempting to maintain? In the final chapter, the author will argue the following: (1) that the only norm provided by the structure and content of Hiltner's model is that supplied by the organism itself; (2) that the form-content distinction to which Hiltner finally resorted is contradicted by the structure and content of his model; and (3) that the conclusions--i.e., those pertaining to the nature and relation of mental and spiritual health--presented by the field theory model are reductionistic and erroneous and thus incorrect in even a preliminary way.

The important issue which must be treated in the following chapter is whether or not it is valid to claim, from a pastoral psychological and/or theological standpoint, that either the form or the content of the salvatory process is fully derived from the isolated organism. In Chapter IV, in light of Hiltner's second model and Clinebell's relational, process-oriented contextual insights, the author will conclude that neither the form nor the content of the salvatory process is fully derived from the isolated organism.

If Hiltner's first model emphasized the process nature and deemphasized the relational nature and context of health and salvation, the opposite is the case with his second model. Processes are approached and differentiated on the basis of their irreducible relational nature. The result, as the structure and content indirectly indicate, is an emphasis on the discontinuity between the salvatory and health processes --see Figure 3 on page 60.

The salvatory process pertains to man's participation in the process of cosmic wholeness. Remaining true to the Biblical terminology, Hiltner states that this participation refers "to man in his true integrity being made derivatively in the image of God, and with the image restored through the person and work of Jesus Christ."[79]

The health process from the Biblical perspective, when

man as an organism or psyche-soma is the focus, refers to the purposive, enabling process. The Bible, Hiltner notes, is not primarily concerned with other types of differentiated knowledge about the nature of organismic health. Its focus is on health as the process of enabling the organism to participate in the salvatory process. Thus the modern focus on biological, medical and psychiatric knowledge is required in order to contribute to an understanding of the full nature of the health process. From the Biblical point of view, as long as the cosmic context is maintained, there is no objection to combining the Biblical and modern concerns.[80]

Health as an enabling process is basic to the health-salvation relation. The relation, however, is complex. Organismic functional wholeness or its restoration does not mean that the individual is either automatically a participant or automatically propelled further along as a participant in the salvatory process. Nor does participation in the salvatory process automatically result in improved organismic functioning. What adequate or improved organismic functioning does mean, according to Hiltner, is that the individual is enabled to participate in that process which is of highest value, cosmic wholeness.[81]

From the standpoint of improvement in health, what is always provided is "a potentiality for progress in the salvatory process."[82] Hiltner resists stating this conversely, a point which will be returned to momentarily. What he means by potentiality for the salvatory process is clarified by his analysis of improvement in health from the perspective of what he had earlier identified as the seven dimensions or "mutually reinforcing and equally indispensable aspects of salvation."[83] According to Hiltner, to be enabled by improvement of health to participate in the salvatory process means dimensionally to be (Hiltner's italics): (1) rescued <u>from</u> limitation of organismic functioning, (2) restored <u>to relatively free functioning</u> , (3) accompanied with <u>positive feeling</u>, (4) released <u>by</u> God in Jesus Christ, (5) unbound <u>in all dimensions of time</u> (i.e., there are consequences for past, present and future), (6) freed for pursuing higher values (i.e., a <u>direction</u> rather than status), and (7) saved <u>as spirit</u>, the object of God's action.[84]

As noted above, Hiltner resists stating that progress in the salvatory process always provides potentiality for increasing organismic health. He apparently is attempting to avoid any confusion between salvation and health as goals when the underlying processes are being considered. His point is that "health exists to serve spirit, not the other way round. More spirit does not necessarily mean more health, provided the health base was relatively adequate to start from."[85] In light of his other qualifying statements, Hiltner clearly does not mean to imply that, in the case of an inadequate health base, spiritual progress necessarily results in more health. At first glance, it would appear that Hiltner's employment of the term "necessarily" is an effort to side-step the issue of potentiality. Upon closer scrutiny, however, it is apparent that Hiltner is drawing the distinction that any potentiality resulting from salvatory advance is only to be regarded as potential for health if improvement in organismic health as a base is needed. In brief, he is consistently maintaining that, from the standpoint of Christian religion, the health process is to function dynamically only in an enabling and never in a competitive capacity with regard to higher values.

Thus the structure and content of the base-value model have successfully provided the corrective for his differentiated organismic approach. By focusing on values or goals, Hiltner has presented a more adequate though more abstract model than his first in attempting to clarify the content significant to pastoral counseling from the healing perspective. At the same time, the differentiated results of his approach, if not considered in conjunction with the relationship-oriented dimensions of mental and spiritual health, perpetuate the danger implicit within his first model, namely, overemphasis on the individual.

Clinebell

With considerable modification of the terms employed by Boisen, Clinebell's model could be characterized from the process standpoint as a unification (ego-oriented integration) -socialization (authentic community) model. As in Boisen's understanding, the structure and content of the personality-in-cosmic-field model indicate that unification and socialization are interdependent--see Figure 4 on page 62. In contrast to Boisen, however, Clinebell approaches both from the standpoint of constructive, reality-oriented, growth-promoting relationships which foster mentally healthy integration and humanizing community.

The unification-socialization process is approached generally in terms of man's fundamental will-to-relate. The needs related to ego development shape the fundamental will-to-relate in need-satisfying ways. The will-to-relate in need-satisfying ways directs man's search for wholeness toward meaningful, fulfilling relationships. In brief, the will-to-relate is a psychosocial bridge concept which focuses attention on man's reality-oriented needs, on the one hand, and those relationship dimensions and dimensions of relationships which are essential for meeting those needs, on the other hand.[86]

The self's reality-oriented relationship-centered needs are understood from the standpoint of what Clinebell considers the one indispensable need (Clinebell's italics): "to experience authentic love in a dependable relationship."[87] All other personality needs are derived from and contribute to the self's capacity to experience the depth giving and receiving of genuine love. These needs are listed as security or stability, service or self-investment in others, esteem or sense of self-respect and worth, enjoyment or constructive and meaningful pleasure, limits or dependable inner structure, freedom or sense of self-directedness and responsibility, and faith or a growth-promoting sense of relatedness to God and the universe.[88] Developmentally, Clinebell concurs with Erik Erikson's understanding of the task-oriented stages of ego development: (1) birth-15 months--basic trust; (2) 15 months-2-1/2 years--autonomy; (3) 2-1/2 years-6/7 years--initiative; (4) 6/7 years-puberty-20 years--identity; (6) young adulthood--intimacy; (7) middle adulthood--generativity; and (8) later years--integrity.[89] Whether viewed from the perspective of child development and the life cycle or that of therapeutic need, Clinebell's model maintains that only in relationships in which genuine love is experienced can persons both meet other basic needs and grow in the capacity to relate in need-satisfying ways. Thus, in Clinebell's words: "Wholeness in the capacity to love is identical with the flowering of mental health."[90]

Boisen, emphasizing conscience development or morality, found socio-psychological categories adequate for illuminating the nature of religious phenomena. Clinebell, focusing on reality-oriented needs and development, has turned to existential psychological and theological as well as psychosocial categories to disclose the religious nature of the participant-observer process. Man's fundamental and irreducible spiritual needs are rooted in the structure of finite man's existence in the universe. To be aware of one's existence is to be conscious of the threat of the self's nonexistence which gives rise to existential anxiety. Closely following Tillich, Clinebell stresses the fact that this form of anxiety is a normal, confronting aspect of human existence which cannot be treated psycho-therapeutically.[91]

From a psychological perspective, the self's personal religion is implicit within his/her response to existential anxiety, for the self's response indicates how the self is attempting to meet spiritual needs and exercise potentially creative personal resources. Psychosocially, the self's response is influenced by and has implications for all interpersonal relationship dimensions.

Clinical experience, according to Clinebell, attests to the fact that all persons have spiritual needs. In his view, the participant self in his/her existential experience and search for full relatedness conveys, with or without awareness, the following spiritual needs:

(1) The need for a meaningful philosophy of life and a challenging object of self-investment.

(2) The need for a sense of the numinous and transcendent.

(3) The need for a deep experience of trustful relatedness to God, other people, and nature.

(4) The need to fulfill the 'image of God' within oneself by developing one's truest humanity through creativity, awareness, and inward freedom.[92]

To deal constructively with existential anxiety requires that the self adequately meet his/her spiritual needs, and to accomplish the latter requires a creative, growth-promoting form of religious thought and practice. In Clinebell's words: "It is with reference to existential anxiety that religion makes its absolutely unique and indispensable contribution to mental health."[93]

The personal resources within man may be utilized destructively as well as creatively. Clinebell stresses the point that the only way man may develop his creative potential and experience his full humanity is within the God-man relationship. Authentic relationship with God is essential for actualizing "that creativity, awareness, and inner freedom which constitute the imago dei."[94] Again it should be noted that Clinebell does not view this form of relationship-oriented growth in perfectionistic terms. The question is rather one of accepting whatever ego-strength and reality-oriented capacity for growth one has.[95] Emphasis is thus placed on the participant observer's acceptance of his/her limitations as well as strengths.

Sin refers to the intrapersonal-interpersonal dimensions of living and relating in self-destructive, irresponsible, non-loving ways.[96] The self is wittingly or unwittingly pursuing an inadequate, non-growth-promoting ultimate. The participant observer's potential for integrating growth is blocked as a result of intrapersonal-interpersonal conflict, the basic cause of which is often self-rejection. Clinebell infers that the dynamic id-superego struggle often underlying sin is an indication of a relationship-deprived weak ego.[97] For the superego to become dominant would only perpetuate the problem. Perfectionism tends to promote a sense of failure and the concomitant need to become engaged in self-punishment and self-rejection.[98] In basic agreement with Hiltner, Clinebell views perfectionism as antithetical to health-promoting religion.

In MENTAL HEALTH THROUGH CHRISTIAN COMMUNITY, Clinebell

states: "Mental health is more of a road than a goal."[99] While Clinebell has always emphasized the process nature of mental-spiritual health, in the study just cited he had not yet fully recognized the implications of his position for understanding the goal in thoroughly process terms. By the time he wrote THE PEOPLE DYNAMIC, however, multidimensional intrapersonal-interpersonal growth in dynamic reality-oriented terms is explicitly visualized as the in-process goal and nature of mental-spiritual wholeness. In brief, that which had escaped Boisen and which Hiltner had been attempting to convey in organismic terms, is brought into clear focus by Clinebell. He states: "Growth results from discovering, affirming, and rejoicing in who one truly is, rather than pursuing an idealized image of what one should be. Becoming takes place by being."[100]

What Clinebell is clearly maintaining is that the mental-spiritual health or wholeness process is not primarily either an individual or social process. Rather it is primarily a constructive, reality-oriented, relationship-centered process, that from which constructive unfication-socialization is derived. In Clinebell's words: "Man is his relationships; the quality of his relationships determines the quality of his mental-spiritual health."[101] Thus, the explicit goal of spiritual growth about which Clinebell speaks is a dimensional relationship-centered, in-process goal. For the individual to be in the process of becoming his/her essential, whole mentally-spiritually healthy self, is for the participant observer to be in life-affirming relationships with self (i.e., ego-oriented integration), others, society, nature and God.

It is clear, then, that the structure and content of Clinebell's model place emphasis on the dynamic, in-process nature of the goal of mental-spiritual wholeness in contrast to perfection. In the following chapter, the author will argue that, by distinguishing between the identifying-with-ideals form of relating and actual reality-oriented relationships, Clinebell, in line with Hiltner's intent, has moved beyond the distortions implicit in Boisen's model.

CHAPTER IV

CONFRONTING THE PROBLEMS AND ISSUES: FINAL ARGUMENTS AND CONCLUSIONS

The task of the present chapter is twofold. First final arguments and conclusions pertaining to those problems and issues brought out by the analysis will be presented. Second, the author will conclude the analysis with a summary of and constructive attempt to embody the emerging directives.

Treatment of the issues will follow treatment of the investigators' problems in each major section and will be presented by stating the primary issue in question form, proceeding with brief discussion, and ending with the author's conclusion.

Fawcett's functional, cognitive and symbolic values will be employed throughout the chapter as needed--the reader is referred to the "Introduction," pages 3 and 4.

Methodological Problems

Problem of Control Model or Theoretical Method

Boisen. Boisen's intended "empirical" theological method, that which he attempted to pursue in an effort to disclose the principles of spiritual life, resulted in relegating mental-spiritual health to a limited-relevance model under the control model of science. His explicit emphasis was placed on exposing the concrete roots of the religious nature of man, those underlying dynamic processes which Freud had failed to understand or interpret adequately. Taken seriously or apart from his hidden assumptions, the author will argue, Boisen's approach necessarily results in methodological reductionism and idolatry.

The charge of misplaced concreteness was insignificant to Boisen because he was approaching the cognitive value of his intended model pragmatically, that is, from the standpoint of the functional and symbolic values of his model. He was convinced, in other words, that if he could describe how faith spontaneously arises from critical problem-solving experiences, actually functions in personal and social life, and is validated in terms of the progressive discriminating socialization-unification process,[1] then the significance and symbolic value of the idea-of-God would be undeniable. As has been elucidated, he carried this program through quite consistently--the distortion entailed will be treated later--interpreting everything pertinent to human development and religion, including man's idea-of-God, in socio-psychological terms.

Unfortunately, the question pertaining to the cognitive value of his model cannot be dispensed with so easily. Boisen was claiming that his method and conclusions were both "empirical" and theological in nature. As a limited-relevance model under the control model of science, his "empirical" or clinical-phenomenological conclusions are subject to the same laws of science as any other empirical findings. Although he modified some of these laws, Boisen himself recognized and accepted this fact.[2]

One such law which Boisen himself employed is the law of economy.[3] According to this widely accepted principle, that least complex theory which accounts for the phenomena is to be accepted as valid. By providing his strong case for the socio-psychological nature of man's idea-of-God (as well as other religious phenomena), Boisen in effect explained away the ultimate ground of this symbol for modern man on the basis of the law of economy. He himself apparently recognized this implication of his method, for he states: "Because of the social utility and therapeutic value of the belief in a personal God, it seems very doubtful whether a purely humanistic religion can ever make any headway outside of university centers."[4] Needless to say, "the social utility and therapeutic value" of belief in God are meaningless to the modern man who accepts Boisen's reductionistic method and conclusions as theological. Religion may have a constructive function and the symbol may work or have a unifying effect in the lives of some people, but the question of what reality the symbol points to is the irreducible cognitive question for modern man.

It should be made clear, furthermore, that Boisen did not intend to promote humanistic religion. As he stated at the close of his study: "It would be indeed a tragedy in my own case if the idea of God did not remain for me something very much more than just a symbol."[5] The point is that Boisen, intending to renew the power of this symbol in particular and theology in general, unwittingly attempted to pursue a method which necessarily reduced theology to science and religion to social psychology. His method is thus reductionistic and idolatrous, for it contributes to the shrinking of reality by explaining away the symbol's ultimate reference. Indeed, the symbol becomes "just a symbol," by which Boisen meant drained of the power derived from its ultimate reference, no longer effective in fostering the leap-of-faith process for modern man. In brief, Boisen's model inadvertently contributes to the demise rather than the revitalization of Christian theology and religion, at most promoting the humanistic religious position he personally eschewed.

Hiltner. In his PREFACE TO PASTORAL THEOLOGY, Hiltner clearly set out to correct and fully develop the potential he found in Boisen's methodology. As his predecessor, he placed emphasis on developing a model which would have functional value. Hiltner, however, was equally concerned that the symbolic and cognitive value of traditional concepts, such as salvation, not be lost as a result of reductionistic method. If a model of healing were to have functional, cognitive and symbolic value, he recognized, it must be developed within a constructive pastoral theological orientation. As the analysis has disclosed, Hiltner was determined to clarify the unique contribution pastoral theology, as a full branch of general theology, might make to both understanding and reception of the faith.

Hiltner's intended emphasis, then, was placed on developing a method which would have the functional value of an operation-centered approach, the cognitive value of a limited-relevance model under the control model of religion, and the symbolic value of pragmatically and clinically sound, non-reductionistic theological results. Clearly he set out to develop, from the standpoint of theoretical method, a thoroughly operation-centered process theology with the context established by the God-man relationship. Man was to be approached from the perspective of the whole organism, and general theological statements were to be interpreted in terms of the underlying processes. However, the key issue for any process theology was totally omitted--i.e., what does the general theological abstraction "God" represent on a process level? As Mickey[6] has also recognized, this has been and continues to be a major hiatus in Hiltner's theoretically-conceived process-oriented theology.[7] In effect, man is thereby removed from the God-man relationship as noted earlier. On the level of theoretical method, then, Hiltner's field theory model, by focusing on the functional and participant-observer nature of the abstracted human organism, is in fact a limited relevance model under a modified form of the scientific control model. Thus Hiltner himself, contrary to his intentions, fell prey to his own brand of methodological reductionism and idolatry. Science was unwittingly labeled theology and central psychobiological healing was labeled religious healing. In short, rather than resolving Boisen's contextual problem, Hiltner magnified its significance.

As brought out earlier in the analysis, Hiltner resolved the control model issue with his base-value model by employing the corrective for which he had provided in PREFACE. However, while the God-man relationship is operative in his second model, no light is shed on the issue of Hiltner's process understanding of God. Hiltner simply relies on the traditional symbols as Biblically given, in this sense extending the validity of Mickey's observation with regard to the smoke-screening effect of Hiltner's appeal to traditional symbols. It is difficult to escape the conclusion that Hiltner's shift in method is an attempt to resolve the contextual problem while circumventing the serious problems raised by his earlier attempt to demonstrate his pastoral theological method.

Clinebell. By approaching the religious control model as primary for pastoral psychology and emphasizing the importance of assimilating all pertinent knowledge gleaned by empirical methods, Clinebell has pursued a theoretical approach congruent with Hiltner's intent. The strength of his method clearly centers in his recognition of the primacy of the religious control model for any limited-relevance model of the nature and relation of mental and spiritual health. However, in his attempt to present a model that brings out the central concerns of religion, Clinebell has been as selective as Boisen with regard to what kinds of knowledge are viewed as pertinent to understanding the nature and relation of mental and spiritual health. In this sense, Hiltner's charge of abstraction is legitimate. As noted earlier, Clinebell places emphasis on the God-personality relationship, the medical aspects of mental health being totally ignored. While disclosure of the functional, symbolic and cognitive value of the God-personality relationship is thereby emphasized, the fact that man is treated one-sidedly deters somewhat from the actual functional value.

Clinebell's theoretical method thus embodies the subtle idealistic inference that psyche is superior to soma. As Hiltner's first model thoroughly indicates, man is always organismic man. As his second model maintains, man in the God-man relationship is still soma and psyche, even if the functional unity of soma and psyche is not to be equated with spirit. From the standpoint of theoretical method, what Clinebell's approach means is that on the one hand, mental health is approached from the significant but limited perspective of differentiated psycho-socio-religious knowledge and, on the other hand, the relation of spiritual health to soma is not treated. As significant as Clinebell's theoretical approach is, then, it detracts from the functional value of treating man in his total organismic nature.

Problem of Operational Method

Boisen. Boisen's employment of the participant-observer method was both highly significant and a serious warning of the dangers entailed in this type of operational method. On the one hand, Boisen was contending that pastoral counselors have as significant a contribution to make to a clinical and phenomenological study of man as do other specialists. He was intent upon exposing the relevance of the participant-observer method for revitalizing theology. If his own theoretical conception of "empirical" theology was a failure, his operational method has provided the significant methodological clue for the development of a practical theology.

On the other hand, Boisen himself was attempting to employ this difficult and potentially troublesome research method, centered as it is in the therapeutic process. Given Boisen's own deep need to balance subjective with objective reality in his own life, the question as to what it meant for Boisen to employ this operational method is highly significant. As has been noted, Boisen knew well what it meant to become lost in the subjective extreme in which idiosyncratic symbols are interspersed with collective symbols. He also had arrived at the insight, via his own experience, that the participant-observer method is itself an affirmation of the unity of reality underlying the extreme approaches of religious participation (with its focus on revelation) and pure empirical science (with its focus on observation and experimentation). He was, in short, both aware of and sensitive to the deep needs of mentally ill persons to become adequate participant observers.

At this point, the more difficult side of the question must be reopened, that pertaining to how adequate a participant observer the pastoral counselor-investigator himself had become. That Boisen made significant progress in coming to grips with his life and making a substantial contribution is undeniable. However, in light of his model of mental and spiritual health as well as the facts of his early development and life course, it is clear that the central thesis running throughout both is perfectionism. It is the author's contention that Boisen's own drive for perfection provides the clue for understanding his own psychopathology, his avoidance of psychoanalysis and his limited understanding of what it means to become an adequate, mentally-spiritually healthy participant observer.

From the standpoint of Boisen's perfectionistic orientation which he himself attempted to justify, the question of whether or not he suffered with an oedipal problem must be left open as one feasible dynamic explanation of the roots of his struggle.[8] The author's primary concern, it should be noted, is not to dabble in clinical speculation, but rather to emphasize the compelling facts pertaining to Boisen's perfectionistic thesis. The point is that Boisen's overemphasis on superego-oriented development, whatever its dynamic roots, was clearly rooted in his own struggle to control primitive impulses. If he interpreted Freud as maintaining the extreme position that cure would follow superego surgery, Boisen himself developed the other extreme position, considering "elimination" of the primitive impulses as one effective alternative, the other being superego-oriented assimilation.[9] Thus, once again, the feasibility of interpreting Boisen's avoidance and apparent fear of psychoanalysis in terms of his early sensitivity to the fact that he was moving in the opposite therapeutic direction than the course a psychoanalyst would be likely to follow, is quite striking.

Be that as it may, Boisen began his work, as has been clarified, with the objective of countering the Freudian understanding of the relation of religion to personality development. As he in his own life tended to identify with ideals rather than form genuine close relationships with others as equals, so he developed a mental-spiritual health model which interprets the adequate participant observer as one who is in process of superego-oriented integration.

The compelling facts, then, tend to lead to the conclusion that Boisen himself did indeed personally become an adequate participant observer in terms of his own understanding. Tragic as it is, Boisen's perfectionistic interpretation of the nature of adequate mentally-spiritually healthy development and religion is invalidated by the clinical facts, including the results of his own pastoral counseling.

Hiltner. In his attempt to advance the pastoral operational method suggested by Boisen's method and work, Hiltner had intended to begin the task of developing a systematic pastoral theology. As has been noted, his intent was to focus on pastoral operations in order to glean theological answers to such questions as the sense in which salvation is a form of healing.

Close examination of Hiltner's chapter on healing (in PREFACE), however, exposes a quite different method operative, one that treats pastoral operations primarily as illustrations of the significance of the organismic approach rather than as the primary content from which theological answers are gleaned. Rather than beginning with and focusing on pastoral operations, Hiltner began with, emphasized and developed his model from the psychobiological interpretation of the differentiated and holistic processes of the functionally whole organism. As Boisen had basically asked what religion and spiritual health mean from his socio-psychological perspective, so Hiltner basically asked what personal religion and spiritual health mean from the perspective of organismic functioning. The result was a psychobiological interpretation of personal religion and salvation. In short, determined to take organismic processes seriously, Hiltner became so immersed in the significant psychobiological material that he lost the pastoral perspective of his own perspectival method.

It should be made quite clear that Hiltner's problem, as disclosed by this analysis, is not that he attempted to bring together the significant findings of cultural disciplines with the contribution of pastoral theology. Rather it is his failure to pursue his operational method, that is, how his focus on the psychobiological material undermined his method, that has emerged from this analysis. If Hiltner was attempting to counter the one-way relationship or discontinuity he found operative in the limited perspective of traditional pastoral care and counseling, i.e., "from the soul to the relationships and problems,"[10] his attempt unwittingly resulted in a one-way relationship in the other direction, overemphasizing continuity between all forms of healing and spirit. Spirit is identified with the psychosomatic unity of the organism as "a unity built up out of the experience of many differentiations."[11]

Between models, Hiltner began his battle to defend his field theory model as correct in a preliminary way.[12] There have been two basic fronts or positions he has been defending, that pertaining to his differentiated organismic approach to mental health, and that pertaining to his organismic approach to spiritual healing. The former has to do with the social dimension of mental health, a problem which will be treated later in this chapter. The latter has to do with whether or not his operational method embodies the fundamental theological context. It is with regard to this latter front that the author intends to show that Hiltner's position vis-a-vis Tillich has been primarily an attempt to defend his first model, and that in the process of doing so, Hiltner himself became increasingly aware of both his actual disagreement with Tillich and the inadequacy of his initial model.

In defense of the theological nature of his model, Hiltner was determined to maintain that his model embodies ultimate as well as preliminary concerns. In one of his earliest attempts to demonstrate his case, Hiltner focused on the role responsibility plays in his model. He argued that responsibility, "at least initially," cannot be considered as a clinical statement because it entails a different level of abstraction: "It is a basic inference about man in his relations to God. . . ."[13] Hence to consider man's responsibility is necessarily to include the God-man relationship as fundamental to the process. To maintain such a position, however, would still require a larger context than the isolated organism.

From Tillich's ontological perspective, Hiltner's field theory model appears to be dealing with man's existence rather than his essence. Hiltner pursued the position that man's 'isness' and 'oughtness' are both treated by science and theology. "In both science and theology the 'ought' and the 'is' are interlaced and in tension in subtle and complex ways."[14] Focusing on the key issue of the relation of psychology to theology, Hiltner distinguished his position from Tillich's by arguing that there is a theological psychology as well as an autonomous discipline of psychology.

> To my position, the stand on psychology as a cultural discipline is like that of Tillich; but my position on psychology as a theological discipline shows it to be internal to theology itself, hence as potentially revelatory of

man's 'essence' as any other branch of theology.[15]

Again, this did not resolve Hiltner's problem, for there is nothing in the field theory model that distinguishes between the autonomous and theological disciplines or indicates theological psychology is actually operative. Thus Hiltner, in an apparent attempt to support the theological nature of his form-content distinction with regard to salvation, presses further: "Whatever may be different about the content, both psychologists and theologians who present serious interpretations of man tend to use a similar structure in relating 'oughtness' to 'isness'."[16] Hiltner is attempting to maintain that the content differs even though the form is the same, a problem central to and thus to be treated in the section pertaining to the structure and content of his model.

In Hiltner's attempt to maintain that in his field theory model he is dealing with man's essence, the key distinction between his and Tillich's position is discernible. Hiltner is attempting to develop a process-oriented interpretation of essence. In doing so, however, he is at the same time attempting to absorb the meaning of the preliminary-ultimate distinction in order to avoid reductionistic conclusions and move beyond the limited way in which ontology approaches concrete organismic processes. Hiltner's point is that "essence," as a strictly ontological term, is "an outworn terminology."[17] In Hiltner's view, it inhibits the kind of two-way dialectic between the actual processes (dynamics) and emerging principles (form) that he considers of major theological significance. Mildly railing at Tillich, Hiltner states:

> The trouble with the ultimate-preliminary distinction is its subtle suggestion that anyone with red blood will be dissatisfied with the preliminary, so why waste time on it at all? To continue using Tillich's terms, I believe, on the contrary, that such vision as we have of the ultimate comes only through our winning through to it by way of the preliminary.[18]

The danger entailed in the fine line that Hiltner is attempting to draw is that if God is identified too closely with human processes, the reverse of his intended method takes place, i.e., theology becomes subsumed under psychology. The implication, of course, is that any pastoral investigator attempting to maintain such a fine line must be exceptionally careful to clarify theoretically and embody operationally his understanding of the nature of the God-man relationship. As has been explicated, that is precisely what Hiltner failed to do in his field theory model.

During the same period that Hiltner was ardently engaged in defending his operation-centered method and resulting model, he was at the same time becoming increasingly aware of the inadequacies entailed in both. With regard to the relation of theoretical to operational method, two studies are particularly revealing. THE CONTEXT OF PASTORAL COUNSELING, written in 1961 by Hiltner and Lowell Colston, places emphasis on relationship-oriented pastoral counseling operations and the goal of salvation.[19] In "Future of Christian Anthropology," Hiltner is again critical of Tillich's ontological approach and "neglect of concrete findings."[20] Of primary significance, however, is his apparent recognition of where he had gotten off the track in his attempt to demonstrate his pastoral theology:

> What you must do is to take into account anything genuinely relevant that turns up from any source. What you must, at all costs, not do is to let your basic criteria of truth, importance, and relevance come from outside the key given by revelation.[21]

Furthermore, following his description of his pastoral theological method, he clarifies what one must methodologically avoid: "first, immersion in the man-science material; second, only then asking what may be its theological significance."[22]

An interspersing of statements in defense of his model with those indicating recognition of the problems with his model appear in "Mental Health and Spiritual Wholeness" (1963). Together with his attempt to further clarify his understanding of organismic functional wholeness, Hiltner states:

> Thus the spirit. . .is the Christian way of talking about what man ought to be--but not as if this were an ideal he had made up. Instead, man is to be or become spirit because that is the basic nature in which God created him. Christians must indeed note that there is a difference between man as he actually is (in truth a sinner) and man as God created him to be. Spirit or spiritual wholeness reminds us, therefore, not so much of what _we_ should try to do, as of what God is _already_ trying to do to work in and through us for our good as well as his.[23]

Hiltner goes on to express further his orthodoxy with regard to the content of man as spirit, shifts back to being "more concrete about spirit and spiritual wholeness,"[24] and then states:

> There is not a perfect and simple correlation between health and spirit, or between mental health and spiritual wholeness.
>
> There is a genuine, although complex, relationship between health and spirit, between mental health and spiritual wholeness.[25]

Thus, it becomes clear that the basic foundation of Hiltner's base-value model had already begun to take shape during the same period he was defending his field theory model. No doubt it was during this period that Hiltner decided to salvage what he could of his initial model by pursuing the course formulated in his phrase, correct "in a preliminary way" (author's italics).

The author is led to the inescapable conclusion that, on the one hand, Hiltner's attempt to defend his first model has been unsuccessful and, on the other hand, Hiltner's self-initiated battle has prompted him to delve more deeply into the nature of both his agreement and disagreement with Tillich's position. Regarding the former, Hiltner has continued to avoid dealing with the process-oriented issues raised by his first model. As has been noted, his second model, while significant as a corrective model, nevertheless has provided Hiltner with a way of circumventing the crucial issues. Had Hiltner reshaped his pastoral theological model, his restoration of focus on relationship-oriented processes would have necessitated some form of the spatial metaphor interpreted constructively. In short, the significant contribution resulting from the reflection on pastoral operations, that which Hiltner initially set out to stress, would have become the actual focus of his model.

It should be noted that Mickey did not evaluate the relation between Hiltner's pastoral theological method and field theory model, the primary focus of the present study. What Mickey tended to imply is correct in a preliminary way, then, explicitly pertains to the two-way pastoral theological method theoretically developed by Hiltner, not to his field theory model.[26]

The author, in basic agreement with Mickey, views Hiltner's theoretical conception of his two-way pastoral theological method as his major and highly significant contribution. It is precisely the significance of his operational method that makes his second attempt to do justice to salvation so disappointing. By backing away from his process-oriented operational method and direct confrontation of the issues, Hiltner has left the impression that the problem lies with the method itself rather than with his own failure to adequately employ it.

Finally, it should not be overlooked that Hiltner's increasing recognition--during the 1960's--of the dangers entailed in employing his method have contributed significantly to the quality of his present understanding of dynamic theology. That he is now prepared to attack the central problem of the process nature of God from his dynamic orientation should indeed be encouraging for those who, as the author, have profitted from Hiltner's contributions.

Clinebell. As is clear from the analysis, Clinebell has avoided the problems that have plagued Boisen and Hiltner by placing emphasis on the pastoral nature of the participant-observer's role as a pastoral counselor-investigator. Rather than attempting either to bracket the pastor's primary religious context or to focus on non-relationship-oriented processes, Clinebell has attempted to take seriously the actual quality of participation in relationships viewed as essential to the process and goal of pastoral counseling. As will be treated in discussion of the issues, it is the multi-dimensional nature of the relationships, that is, pastoral counselor-God-counselee(s) which underscores the operational pervasiveness of the theological psychology Hiltner has disclosed as of fundamental significance to a process orientation.

Analogical-Descriptive Model Problem

Boisen. Boisen's methodological problems were all rooted in his failure to recognize the actual nature and limitations of his work. As has been disclosed, his imperialistic approach to "empirical" theology was the result of his metaphysical approach to science rather than a scientific approach to theology. His methodological optimism was clearly rooted in his idealistic metaphysics which influenced all of his work. Thus for Boisen, to be descriptive of empirical reality was to engage in the significant task of identifying and describing the teleological nature of human evolution in its movement toward its Absolute Source. The purportedly descriptive socio-psychological findings were highly significant to him because he was thoroughly convinced that only the blind would fail to recognize God's immanence in the brilliant socialization-unification design.

What Boisen was intending to do was describe empirically sound theological principles in order to counter Freud's interpretation of religion. In light of the way his idealistic perspective influenced his work, it is clear that Boisen's method and conclusions were as normative as Freud's. If Freud fell prey to one extreme in identifying sick religion as generic, Boisen succumbed to the opposite extreme in assuming that religion, whatever its form and content, has an essential positive function. Thus, ironically, Boisen's approach is theological, but it is no more capable of attaining thoroughly descriptive results than Freud's approach. The author must conclude that Boisen was unwittingly misusing his purportedly descriptive method to justify his own faith position. His failure to recognize the actual theological, model-constructing nature of his work clearly prevented him from developing an adequate analogical model.

Hiltner and Clinebell. Both Hiltner and Clinebell, on the other hand, recognized that they could only be as descriptive as possible within the context of an analogical model. The criteria they employed in selecting their stated or implied analogical models, however, vary considerably.

In selecting his first model, Hiltner focused on the capacity of the magnet-and-files field theory metaphor for conveying the human organismic processes from the standpoint of both differentiated and holistic healing. He found the field theory model uniquely suitable for avoiding what he considered the spatial problem, on the one hand, and exposing the continuity of all forms of healing, on the other. It avoided the internal spatial problem by conveying, in line with the modern perspectival approach to the organism, that the personality and person-centered dimensions of processes together form one way of viewing the total organism. At the same time, the magnet as focus of the magnetic field, representing the organized personality, provided the means for emphasizing that which is central to Christian or salvatory healing without categorically separating it from other forms of healing. He was convinced in brief, that the field theory model had the capacity to relate the modern health-related findings of the cultural disciplines to the time-tested insights of religion. In Hiltner's view, it provided an exceptional way to embody his pastoral theological principle of two-way dialogue, that which he maintained was fundamental to his method.

What Hiltner failed to recognize was that his modern assumptions had focused his attention on non-theological criteria for selecting his model. The significant concern he was emphasizing was how to disclose the continuity between all forms of healing. That which is distinctive about religious healing was unwittingly dispensed with on the modern grounds that the goal is organismic integration.

In contrast to the criteria employed in selecting his first model, the criteria operative in the selection of his second model were quite different. Those criteria which ostensibly had been primary to the development of his first model, demonstration of his pastoral theological method and concomitant development of a process-oriented pastoral model, were set aside in favor of what he had labeled a logic-centered approach. The main criteria for selecting the base-value analogy, as indicated earlier in the study, were (1) its capacity to correct his earlier conclusions, and (2) to do so without deemphasizing the significance of his organismic orientation. It provided the means for avoiding the problem he had brought upon himself with his first model.

That criterion which focused on restoring the God-man relationship as central to Hiltner's theological understanding of the nature and relation of mental and spiritual health, was the determinative criterion of selection for Clinebell's model. The difference is that Clinebell has derived his understanding of which processes are primary, and thus his model, from the religious control model itself. The primary criterion, then, was provided by the ultimate relationship. The way man was to be treated was governed by his relationship-oriented nature disclosed by the God-man relationship. Clearly the fundamental criterion is that pastoral psychology and theology must begin with its own unique contribution as primary, and all other contributions from the mental health-related disciplines as significant but secondary.

Methodological Issues

Theoretical Method

Primary issue. In approaching the task of mental-spiritual health model-building, what is entailed in theoretically maintaining the distinctive nature of the religious control model?

Discussion. As the analysis has disclosed, three general contextual criteria are entailed in approaching mental-spiritual health models from a pastoral psychological and/or theological perspective: (1) the God-man relationship must be considered essential and irreducible; (2) God must be taken seriously; (3) and man must be taken seriously. As the author will attempt to clarify, the symbolic, functional and cognitive values of mental-spiritual health models are functions of the above three criteria. In other words, to the extent that the three criteria are operative, to that extent the model will manifest these values. That the three contextual criteria are interrelated is self-evident, yet as has been exposed by the analysis, the meaning of these criteria for pastoral psychology and/or theology has not always been understood by the model-builders themselves.

The first and primary criterion means that the man-God relationship itself is what must be considered concrete reality for pastoral counselor-investigators. It is this criterion which determines what contributions from other fields are relevant as well as how they may be used in the mental-spiritual health model-building task. It also determines what may and may not be carried out operationally. From the standpoint of the shepherding process, the nature of the God-man relationship implicit within the pastoral counselor's understanding of mental-spiritual health and modes of conveying same, may serve to facilitate or impede growth-promoting faith. Thus, constructively or destructively, it may have major symbolic value for those engaged in the shepherding relationship.

The primary nature of the God-man relationship requires that both sides of it be considered with equal seriousness from the relationship orientation. The two secondary criteria place emphasis on the fact that the potential symbolic value of the central relationship for any theological model is enhanced only when man in his full irreducible nature (psychosoma or organismic self) and God in his full ultimate nature (transcendent and immanent Ground or Spirit, however specifically interpreted theologically) are considered essential to the relationship. From the standpoint of the shepherding process, the functional value of the nature of man (human potentiality) and cognitive value of the nature of God (ultimate actuality) implicit within the pastoral counselor's conveyance of his mental-spiritual health perspective are of major consequence. They may largely determine the extent to which mediation of mental-spiritual health will take place.

Clearly all three contextual criteria are essential for pastoral psychological and/or theological model-constructing, and their adequacy is assessed by the extent to which the resulting models they shape manifest functional, cognitive and symbolic value. In other words, only when all three criteria are taken seriously is the resulting model as a whole capable of constructively embodying the full distinctive nature of the religious control model, that which is essential to its functional, cognitive and symbolic value.

Conclusion. The crucial nature of this issue for the development of a pastoral psychological and/or theological model has been brought out by the analysis. Ironically, the two investigators who explicitly stated that they intended to focus on doing theology were those who succumbed to methodological reductionism and idolatry. Hiltner's eventual recognition of this fact and correction of his theoretical problem serve as a significant warning to operation-oriented pastoral investigators who intend to take theological issues seriously in nonreductionistic terms.

While the issue for many modern pastoral psychologists and theologians may well be the meaning of the central symbol of God, the theoretical methodological issue stresses only that the investigator, whatever his theological persuasion, embody the God-man relationship as central and irreducible to his mental-spiritual health model, on the one hand, and recognize the continuity between and significance of the functional, cognitive and symbolic values of his relationship-oriented model, on the other hand. Hence the potential healing significance of pastoral psychological and theological model-building itself, that to which Clinebell--of the three investigators considered--has been the most sensitive, is at stake.

Finally, precisely because of the importance of the ultimate relationship, the significant task of exposing its relevance is one to which, as Hiltner has disclosed, pastoral psychologists and theologians have much to contribute. Thus from the perspective of mental-spiritual health models, the significance of being open to and informed about all findings relevant to man as well as sensitive to the pertinent clinical-phenomenological material regarding man's conceptions of God is underscored when the religious control model provides the context.

Operational Method

Primary issue. What may the pastoral counselor-investigator legitimately study or investigate?

Discussion. Once the meaning and significance of taking the religious control model seriously is grasped, that which the pastoral counselor-investigator may legitimately study comes into clear focus. From the perspective of mental-spiritual health, it is man's total relationship-oriented nature, that which has its Ground, meaning and in-process fulfillment within the authentic God-man relationship, that is the focus both of the shepherding process and pastoral investigations.

As all three investigators have brought out or implied, the participant-observer operational method is of fundamental significance for understanding the general nature of the therapeutic task and goal as well as the pastoral counselor's role. The participant-observer nature of the task and goal center in the capacity of both the pastoral counselor and counselee(s), via their relationship, to become increasingly aware of and responsive to who they are and who God is in the actual relating taking place.

The pastoral counselor-investigator, then, as a participant in and observer of actual relationships, legitimately investigates what is entailed in mental and spiritual health-promoting and health-inhibiting forms of relating. All relationship-oriented questions become pertinent, not only to the counseling situation, but to the nature of ministry and the humanization process in general. What are the pastoral counselor's and counselee's relationships to self, others (including the counselee/pastoral counselor), society (including the church), nature and God? Is the pastoral counselor open, sensitive and responsive to the needs of the counselee and prepared, in terms of his/her own personal development, to enter a growth-promoting, health-enhancing relationship? What God is the pastoral counselor mediating in the relationship and is the counselee responding to or rejecting?

It becomes clear that, in the author's view, it is Clinebell's mental-spiritual health model that is most dialogically shaped by and contributive to his understanding of relationship-oriented pastoral counseling. As such, it promotes, on the process level, the kind of theological psychology and two-way dialogue which has the capacity to move toward the discernment of psycho-socio-religious bridge categories of primary significance for an adequate interpretation of the humanization process.

Conclusion. If both mental and spiritual health are primarily, from the in-process or functional standpoint, experienced in, through and for relationships, then the total human organism in all its reality-oriented relationships is what the pastoral counselor as pastoral counselor-investigator may legitimately study.

Analogical-Descriptive Models

Primary issue. What specific criteria are to be employed in the selection of an adequate analogical model of the nature and relation of mental and spiritual health?

Discussion. As has surfaced from the analysis, every mental-spiritual health model is necessarily an analogical model developed as a limited-relevance model under some control model. When this fact is recognized, and when the theological significance of developing a mental-spiritual health model under the control model of religion is understood, then the valuational relevance of the analogical model the pastoral counselor-investigator selects becomes obvious.

The relation of this question to the control model issue should by now be clear. To take the religious control model seriously means that the pastoral counselor-investigator is limited in the specific criteria he may employ in selecting an adequate analogical model. The two specific criteria which must be employed from the standpoint of pastoral psychology and/or theology are: (1) the primacy of the theological relationship-oriented process, and (2) the valuational process implicit to the content of mental-spiritual health.

What the first criterion means is that the analogical model selected must have the capacity to focus on the theological relationship-oriented process. What the second criterion means is that the metaphor selected must also be capable of embodying the valuational process the investigator considers sound on the basis of his clinical, phenomenological and theological understanding. These two criteria are interrelated as the analysis has disclosed. For Boisen, the socialization-unification valuational process, a la Mead, followed from his failure to shape his analogical model in line with the religious control model. For Hiltner, the organismic valuational process that he employed, a la Goldstein and Rogers, followed from his failure to pursue and select an analogical model to embody the relationship-oriented shepherding process. For Clinebell, the psycho-socio-religious valuational process, a la Sullivan and Tillich, omitting the psychobiological dimension, followed from his use of an analogical model selected to embody the relationship dimensions and dimensions of relationships he views as central to the meaning of mental-spiritual health. Thus, both specific criteria must be taken into consideration in the selection process.

Conclusion. The two specific criteria essential for selecting an adequate analogical model are derived from the religious control model. Clearly the choice of an analogical model on the basis of the primacy of the theological relationship-oriented process and concomitant valuational process is of major symbolic, functional and cognitive significance.

Problems with Content and Structure of Models

Problem of Embodying the Relational Nature of and Relation of Mental-Spiritual Health

Boisen. Corresponding to his reductionistic method, the structure and content of Boisen's socialization-unification or personality-in-social-field model resulted in the reductionistic conclusion that mental health and salvation are identical. Boisen was not cognizant of the fact that he had methodologically ruled out any differentiation between these concepts. While he recognized that his dynamic socio-psychological orientation totally determined the relational nature of mental and spiritual health embodied by the structure and content of his model, he erroneously was convinced that the significance of his findings would point to that ultimate Intelligence transcending all methods.

As has been explicated, the central problem for understanding the relational nature of mental or spiritual health, in Boisen's view, was that of the relation of the individual to society or socialization. It was the balance between individual interests and interests of the group that must be maintained on the basis of the clinical-phenomenological facts. In his view, Freud had failed to take the clinical-phenomenological material seriously due to his own biases. Boisen's own attempt to do so, however, resulted in a model the structure and content of which distorted the very balance he desired to establish.

Not only was Boisen's preferred term, "conscience," a poor choice to represent his interpretation of the nature of personal and social wholeness; his interpretation failed to fully grasp the reality-oriented nature of genuine relationships. As will be further clarified in the following problem section, idealizations and movement toward becoming perfect focus on the kind of part-process self-relation which the depth psychological tradition and constructive theology have identified as a major source of man's difficulties--the over-controlling superego, god-complex or idolatry. The author must conclude that Boisen's identifying-with-ideals approach to the nature of relationships in general and the God-man relationship in particular resulted in an inadequate, imbalanced interpretation of what constitutes spiritual wholeness. As the structure and content of his model indicate, then, from the relational standpoint, Boisen's understanding of the self-relation and concomitant relational nature of mental/ spiritual health is basically nothing more than an attempt to promote displacement of the ego by the superego, and to establish the latter as the center of personality integration.

Hiltner. The primary problem with Hiltner's organismic field theory model is its total failure to embody the relational nature and relation of mental and spiritual healing or health. Hiltner's strength, his consistent attention to and deliberating examination of the concrete organismic processes, became his vulnerability to the seductive lure of the organismic integration process. He had intended to demonstrate the significance of a pastoral theological method which recognizes and attempts to remain true to the integral dialectical process nature of ultimate and preliminary concerns. Somewhere in the process--if the author may be permitted this appropriate word play--Hiltner became a victim of his own overemphasis on the differentiated concrete findings, the result being his losing sight of the relational nature of mental and spiritual health.

Thus from the relational standpoint, the structure and content of Hiltner's first model are totally ineligible for treating the nature and relation of mental and spiritual healing. Spirit, a relationship-oriented category as Hiltner himself has subsequently recognized, is equated with organismic categories, the result being that spiritual healing is reduced to mental healing organismically conceived. At most, then, Hiltner's model is a secular psychobiological model of total health as functional wholeness.

The structure and content of Hiltner's base-value model, on the other hand, embody the relational nature of and clearly differentiate between organismic health and salvation as base and highest values, respectively. His second model, though not a process-centered model, corrects the contextual problem with his earlier model.

Finally, it must be noted that both of Hiltner's models are partial models, focusing on and overemphasizing the dynamic differentiated organismic nature of integrating forms of healing within or outside of the God-man relationship. That mental health entails social relatedness as well as intra-organismic relatedness is not denied, it is merely not treated in either model.[27] The valuational-significance problem with the partial-model approach implied earlier and to be further discussed under relation-oriented issues applies to both of Hiltner's models. Rather than belabor the point, the author will here conclude that both of Hiltner's models, significant as they are from the standpoint of differentiated knowledge, are of limited pastoral theological significance due to the fact that they are partial models.

Clinebell. The structure and content of Clinebell's model adequately convey the relational nature of and relation to mental and spiritual health. His model does lack the necessary structure, however, to treat man's full organismic nature adequately. That man is more than a personal self-relation is not insignificant to the full relationship-oriented self-acceptance, self-affirmation and self-actualization Clinebell's model intends to promote.

Problem of Embodying the Process Nature of Mental-Spiritual Health

Boisen. From the process perspective, the analysis has disclosed, the structure and content of Boisen's model focus on conscience development as the central religious function and goal of individual and social evolution. The author has argued that Boisen's own deep personal needs drove him to attempt to control his sexual impulses by establishing the superego in control of the personality, and as is often if not always the case with counselors in general, Boisen's own problems led to his operational insights as well as limitations. Here the author will argue that it was the combination of his deep personal needs reinforced by his theological orientation that solidified Boisen's dynamic understanding of mental or spiritual health, preventing him from recognizing the destructive imbalance captured by the structure and content of his model.

The fact that Boisen's purportedly bracketed idealistic metaphysics were infused into his supposedly descriptive socio-psychological interpretations not only nullifies his "empirical" claim; it also throws further light on why he found no difficulty with his perfectionistic interpretation of personality. It is clear that his identification of an essential function of religion, that which he integrally associated with the evolvement of conscience, is rooted in his metaphysical understanding of the progressive movement of mental emergents toward their source in Absolute Mind. To establish superego-oriented integration is to participate in the religious task of actualizing the highest conceivable ideals in personal and social life. It is to promote that kind of humanization process in which creative socialization results in creative unification. For Boisen, both on theoretical and clinical-phenomenological grounds, the superego represented an all-inclusive emergent capable of characterizing the dynamic integration of the whole, ultimate purpose-promoting person and social group.

The structure and content of Boisen's model expose the contradiction within his dynamic understanding. If ideals determine what is and is not to be integrated, then repression of what the individual finds unacceptable is unwittingly fostered. The ideal goal focuses man's attention on striving to be that which man is not, perfect. Forgiveness, which Boisen recognized as being of primary significance,[28] is then unacceptable because the superego-centered person can neither accept or forgive self nor accept the acceptance and forgiveness of God and other persons. Identification with ideals thus takes the place of genuine relating, and the process is exposed as the idolatrous attempt to become God.

Thus the author must further conclude that Boisen's own reaching out, both personally and theoretically, for the dynamic experience and understanding of spiritual wholeness was delimited by his experience of what worked for him--i.e., imbalanced superego-centered personality--reinforced by his idealistic theological position.

Hiltner. The content and structure of Hiltner's field theory model clearly indicate his exclusive emphasis on the dynamics of organismic integration. Hiltner attempted to outdo Boisen in his avoidance of presenting conclusions in abstract, non-process terms. As has been elucidated, Hiltner insisted that organismic processes be finally understood from the holistic standpoint. Thus his conclusions are presented in terms of the nature of the concrete, attainable organismic process goal of over-all functional wholeness, not in terms of an abstracted personality and unattainable ideal self.

The primary problem Hiltner faced with regard to his organismic process model, however, was how to embody the religious norm for decision-making and holistic salvatory healing. As brought out in an earlier section of the analysis, Hiltner was forced to turn to the abstract form-content distinction in a final attempt to avoid the reductionistic conclusion that spiritual healing or health is synonymous with organismic healing or healthy psychosomatic functioning. However, as the analysis has indicated, the structure of a model limits the nature of the content embodied. Once he committed himself to the structure and content of the field theory model, no form-content distinction not already given by the metaphor could be substantiated.

Since in the magnet-and-files metaphor there is a simple direct correlation between any change in the magnet and change in the files, the model is only capable of bringing out the continuity between all forms of healing. That, as has been noted, was one of the major reasons Hiltner selected the metaphor to begin with. The form-content distinction, then, is contradicted by the structure and corresponding content of the model itself. Thus the only norm embodied by the structure and content of Hiltner's field theory model is that supplied by the isolated organism.

Hence the conclusion that the field theory model's interpretations of the nature and relation of mental and spiritual health are reductionistic and erroneous is here reinforced. The author is compelled to conclude that there is no sense in which Hiltner's organismic process model may be legitimately construed as correct.

Clinebell. In contrast to Boisen's intended model and Hiltner's first model, the structure and content of Clinebell's model, as the analysis of same has disclosed, focus on the multidimensional nature and centrality of the in-process goal of the God-man relationship. From the process perspective, the only problem with Clinebell's model is the lack of structure and content to include man's full dynamic, organismic process nature. The model's dynamic strength, that which will be discussed further under process-related issues, is the capacity of its structure and content to embody the meaning of mental-spiritual wholeness in non-reductionistic terms.

Issues Pertaining to Structure and Content

Relational Nature of Mental and Spiritual Health

Primary issue. From the perspective of the relational nature of and relation of mental and spiritual health, what is the pastoral psychological and/or theological significance of the structure and content of partial models?

Discussion. As the analysis has disclosed, the mental-spiritual model-constructing task of pastoral psychology and/or theology is partly descriptive and partly normative. Two-way dialogue between the theological relationship-oriented context and content and the clinical and empirical content from the cultural disciplines is essential if the full nature of the God-man relationship is to be adequately treated. In short, some descriptive-in-normative-context interpretation of what it means to form a mentally-spiritually healthy, whole self-relation is necessarily embodied by the structure and content of pastoral psychological and/or theological models. A balanced reality-oriented perspective is required if the model is to embody adequate functional, cognitive and symbolic value.

Overemphasis on differentiated descriptive knowledge, then, is not without normative implications and vice versa. Any tendency, implicit within the structure and content of a model, to overdifferentiate or overemphasize detracts from the theological significance of the model.

Conclusion. If the pastoral theological task is one of promoting "the reception and assimilation of faith,"[29] as Hiltner maintains it is, and if relationship-oriented wholeness is the in-process goal, then all partial models, inadequate as they are for providing the required balance and perspective, are of limited theological significance.

Process Nature of Mental and Spiritual Health

Primary issue. From the perspective of the process nature of mental-spiritual health, what is the pastoral psychological and/or theological significance of the structure and content of perfectionistic models?

Discussion. At this stage of the analysis, it should be apparent to the reader that this issue is closely correlated with the issue of partial models. What the analysis has disclosed with regard to the perfection versus wholeness issue, is that perfection-oriented models are both psychologically and theologically unsound because they fail to grasp the nature of either the concrete reality-centered, relationship-oriented processes or the mentally-spiritually healthy self-relation.

Pressing this issue to its limits, however, the question that arises is whether some form of perfection is not necessarily entailed in the salvatory goal, such as perfect wholeness or the perfect God-man relationship. What the analysis has disclosed is that spiritual wholeness is a reality-centered in-process goal derived from the primary in-process goal of human life, namely, relationship with God. In the author's view, this is the most significant and perhaps least understood finding of pastoral psychology and/or theology to date with regard to the dynamic nature of mental-spiritual health. As the analysis has brought out, it means that perfect wholeness, perfect God-man relationship or any other form of perfection referring to man or his relationships is psychologically and theologically a contradiction in terms. The in-process goal of spiritual wholeness becomes a living reality or experience for man when all striving-after-perfection and idealization-centered forms of relating cease and genuine or authentic relationship with God[30] begins.

Conclusion. The author must conclude that what the structure and content of all perfectionistic mental-spiritual health models embody is necessarily, from the perspective of pastoral psychology and/or theology, a partial, imbalanced and destructive interpretation of both relationship-centered processes and the whole self-relation.

Summary and Constructive Consideration of Emerging Directives

In this final section of the analysis, the author will attempt to briefly summarize the emerging directives and consider their embodiment in a comprehensive mental-spiritual health model.

Summary of Emerging Directives

Methodologically, several precise directives have emerged for clarifying what theoretical and operational procedures may and may not be pursued in the development of a nonreductionistic pastoral psychological and/or theological model of the nature and relation of mental and spiritual health.

First, the religious control model must be theoretically and operationally maintained. As has been explicated, what this means is that the primary norm for a pastoral psychological and/or theological model is the God-man relationship itself. It is the God-man relationship which must govern all theoretical and operational procedures.

Second, from the standpoint of mental-spiritual health model-building, the relationship-oriented norm requires that both sides of the primary relationship be treated seriously and comprehensively in order to take the full meaning of "relationship" seriously. All differentiated knowledge relevant to human health and wholeness from whatever source is to be approached as significant.

Third, in light of the above two directives, mental-spiritual health model-building must be approached comprehensively though within the limits of the limited-relevance, analogical nature of the task. While pastoral psychology and theology must always be aware of its perspectival nature, i.e., that it is but one approach among many for understanding the nature of Judeo-Christian faith, it must approach its limited-relevance function comprehensively in order to do justice to the theological nature of its task. In other words, the pastoral counselor-investigator must take into consideration the irreducible symbolic, functional and cognitive value manifest in his/her method and developing model.

From the standpoint of the structure and content of a nonreductionistic mental-spiritual health model, several corresponding directives surface.

First, man's fundamental relationship-oriented nature, as disclosed by the God-man relationship, must be considered of primary significance in and of itself for understanding the pastoral psychological and theological interpretation of mental and spiritual health as processes. All relationship dimensions of man's life are thus viewed as having a religious dimension. To be comprehensive, therefore, the structure and content of a mental-spiritual health model must be capable of including all relationship dimensions entailed in the humanization process.

Second, the structure and content of a comprehensive model must take man's full organismic or psychosomatic nature seriously. Mental and spiritual health as derived from the God-man relationship refer to different dimensions of the total psychosoma in the relationship. Thus the structure and content of the selected model must have the capacity to fully embody and value, within the relationship context, the somatic as well as psychological aspects of the organism.

Finally, the structure and content must have the capacity to convey the possibility of discontinuity as well as continuity between mental and spiritual health in order to avoid any misleading implication that there is a simple direct correlation between these processes.

The above summary of emerging directives stresses the fact that there must be continuity between theoretical and operational method, on the one hand, and between method and developing model, on the other. As has become clear by the analysis, this means that no part of the process of pastoral model-constructing is to be construed as non-theological. In this author's view, then, the on-going pastoral psychological and theological model-constructing task is to be understood in terms of the development of a comprehensive model, one increasingly providing an adequate, self-validating interpretation of the psychobio-socio-religious nature of the humanization process. As such, it will move beyond past limitations and increasingly develop in its capacity to embody symbolic, functional and cognitive value.

Constructive Attempt to Embody Emerging Directives

A brief prefatory comment on method is perhaps overdue. The astute reader will have noted that the format for this analysis may be construed as ontologically biased due to the fact that form (relational nature) precedes dynamics (process nature).[31] The actual emphasis that all three investigators have attempted to maintain, though not always constructively from the theological standpoint, is that which the author has intended to promote constructively, namely, the unity between form and dynamics. The point is that this is a pastoral psychological and theological assumption in itself, one that has significance for understanding the symbolic as well as functional and cognitive value of mental-spiritual health models.

If the form and dynamics are viewed as two perspectives on the same relationship-oriented processes, then ontological and process categories are recognized as two perspectives on the same reality. It is then not a matter of form preceding dynamics or dynamics preceding form, but rather the juxtaposition of and dialectical tension between form and dynamics. It would appear that all three investigators, but especially Hiltner and Clinebell, have been attempting to clarify this important point.

The model which embodies the emerging directives is best characterized as an organismic-self-in-cosmic-field model--see Figure 5. It represents a synthesis of the significant findings of Hiltner and Clinebell (and Boisen via both) while attempting to overcome the problems and seriously treat the issues emerging from the analysis.

In line with the process orientation of all three investigators, the organismic-self-in-cosmic-field model attempts to expose the primary relationship-oriented processes from the pastoral psychological and theological perspective. In accord with Clinebell's recognition of the dimensional centrality of the God-man relationship, mental-spiritual health is primarily understood from the standpoint of the relationship dimensions and dimensions of relationships. It is the whole functioning organismic self, however, who is the relater in each relationship dimension.

It should be noted that the organismic self is not represented by the magnet-and-files field theory metaphor. The latter is dispensed with on the theological and psychological grounds that it overemphasizes continuity and is incapable of conveying the actual discontinuity that may be present between mental and spiritual dimensions of healing and health.

It is the direct correlation between magnet and field that contributed to Hiltner's erroneous conclusions. By removing that which implies automatic change rather than potentiating effect, which requires replacing the field theory metaphor with different structure--i.e., dots as personality potential, pluses as somatic aspects, and horizontal and vertical arrows as centered personality--to emphasize the empowering nature of actualizing one's personality potential, the problem is resolved without losing sight of Hiltner's intent. The ego-centering, integrating actualization of personality potential represented by the arrows thus indicates that the self-relation is primarily an intrapersonal-interpersonal relationship-oriented self-identity, that which is empowered by and for the organismic-self-in-all-reality-oriented-relationships. The mentally-spiritually healthy organismic self is thus viewed from both the perspective of the personality-potential-being-actualized process and the perspective of the somatic aspects. With regard to the latter, progress in the mental-spiritual health process empowers the total organism to effect whatever changes are possible. The fact that discontinuity may be present between these process dimensions is thus embodied by the structure and content of the model.

As Hiltner and Clinebell would agree, the organismic self may have some irreversible disease, such as an irremovable brain tumor, affecting the whole organism, and yet be adequately moving in the spiritual health process. Life may not have lost its meaning and purpose; that is to say, the God-man relationship may still be central to the individual's life. On the other hand, the organismic self may, from the functional organismic standpoint, have a measure of mental health which lacks the capacity for constructive intrapersonal-interpersonal empowerment precisely because the spiritual dimension is underdeveloped or is being developed in relation to an inadequate ultimate.

From the standpoint of that which is essential and central to both mental and spiritual health, the God-man relationship, this intrapersonal-interpersonal empowerment model emphasizes the in-process goal of wholeness expressed in the capacity to love. In terms of man's self-relation, what this means is that ego-oriented integration is empowered by that ultimate Ground in relationship to which self-identity[32] is affirmed and fostered. What is derived from the God-man relationship, then, is aptly described as spiritual wholeness, for it entails that which empowers the participant-observer to constructively accept, affirm and love his/her total organismic self within and for all relationships. In brief, the purpose and meaning derived from the reality-oriented, wholeness-promoting relationship with God form that which is an essential empowering stimulus for the organismic-self-in-process-of-becoming.

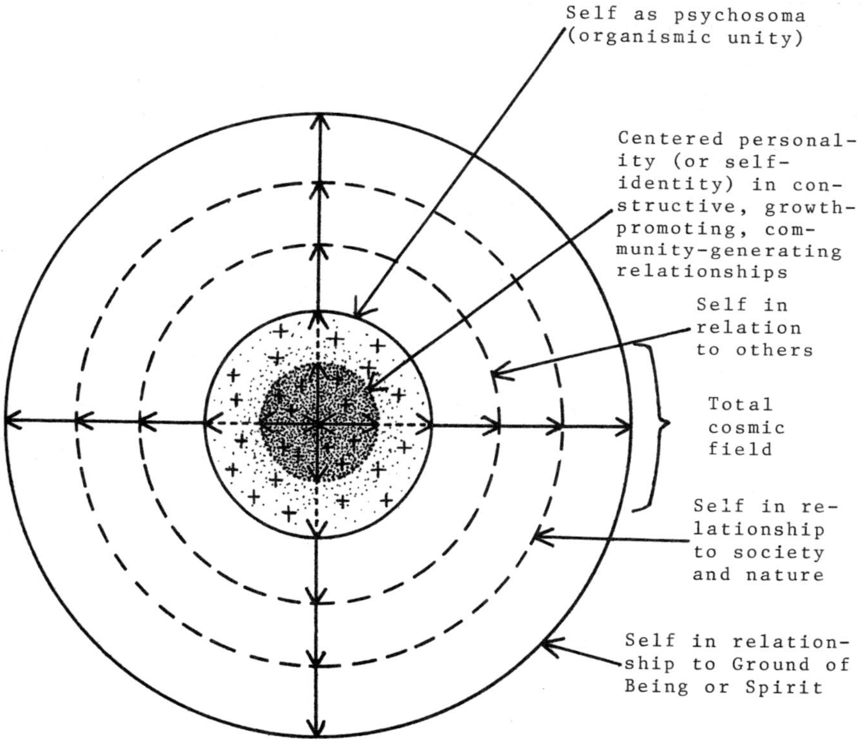

Figure 5. A longitudinal spherical cross-section of the comprehensive, multidimensional, relationship-oriented model of mental-spiritual health emerging from the analysis, representing personality potential with dots, the actualized centered personality with the intrapersonal arrows, the somatic aspects of the organism with plus signs (+'s), the relationship dimensions of positive mental health with concentric circles, the horizontal and vertical dimensions of each relationship with the horizontal and vertical lines, and the process nature of mental-spiritual health with arrows

Again, the unconditional Love of God experienced by the participant-observer, even when received in the sense of forgiveness and affirmation, do not automatically mean that all of the organismic self's problems are resolved. It may and often does mean that the organismic self is freed to identify problems never before recognized. It may also mean, as in the case of Paul's blindness following his conversion experience, that transitional problems are a necessary part of the traumatic nature of the personality transformation taking place.

In concluding this study, the author must again reiterate that the mental-spiritual health model emerging from the directives is in no sense to be considered as a final model. It is rather, if this analysis has been carried out adequately, an indication of the present development of pastoral psychology and theology. The ongoing task, in this author's view, is the development of an increasingly adequate, comprehensive model, one which possesses the kind of heuristic intent, depth of insight and balance that is functionally enabling, cognitively convincing, and symbolically compelling.

FOOTNOTES

PREFACE

[1]As is commonly accepted in the literature of pastoral psychology and theology, "spiritual health" will be employed in this study as a synonym for salvation. It should be noted, however, that Seward Hiltner has become critical of this usage--an issue which will be treated later in this study.

[2]Except in those instances when the context clearly indicates otherwise, the terms "problem" and "issue" are assigned technical meanings in the analysis of the models. "Problem" refers to an inconsistency rooted in an investigator's intended and/or actual methodological approach to his model(s) or the structure and content of that model(s). "Issue," on the other hand, refers to a differentiated question requiring treatment in any serious pastoral psychological and/or theological consideration of the nature and relation of mental and spiritual health.

[3]In the case of Boisen, whose autobiography indicates the correlation between most of his life and the development of his mental health-salvation model, the author has found it necessary to be even more selective, for the most part including only major influences and events.

[4]Paul Johnson, Carroll Wise, Wayne Oates and Russell Dicks all deserve mention. Paul Johnson's contribution, which focused on the nature of healthy intrapersonal and interpersonal development, was an early and somewhat naive attempt to bridge the gap between various schools of psychology by bringing them into a synthesis congenial to theology. As was Hiltner, Wise and Oates were students of Boisen who have followed his leads. Both have made significant contributions to the understanding of the nature of mental health, Wise in terms of a psychosomatic viewpoint and Oates in terms of his theological orientation. Dicks, who has extended Cabot's "healing force" concept into a basic theory of health in TOWARD HEALTH AND WHOLENESS (New York: Macmillan, 1960), has focused on practical concerns and tended to avoid the more difficult theoretical issues.

More recent contributors roughly considered of Clinebell's generation are James Lapsley, Don Browning and Edward Thornton. Lapsley and Browning, former students of Hiltner--Lapsley is presently Hiltner's colleague at Princeton Theological Seminary--have both contributed to Hiltner's approach in their early publications. Lapsley's most recent book, SALVATION AND HEALTH: THE INTERLOCKING PROCESSES OF LIFE (Westminster, 1972)--the author read Lapsley's study in galley form during the time the present analysis was being carried out--presents a significant process model which deserves special attention. Thornton, a former student of Oates, introduces his constructive pastoral theological position--in THEOLOGY AND PASTORAL COUNSELING (Englewood Cliffs: Prentice-Hall, 1964)--which he has found helpful for throwing light on some of the major problems. All three of these men have proven themselves to be significant contributors.

[5]Edward Thornton, PROFESSIONAL EDUCATION FOR MINISTRY (Nashville: Abingdon, 1970), 55-71.

[6]Wayne Oates, "Quintessential," CHRISTIAN CENTURY, 72 (November 16, 1955), 1339.

[7]Few men living or deceased belong to the select club of those to whom four books have been dedicated. Hiltner has been honored with membership in this club as indicated by the dedication of the following studies: THE NATURE OF MAN, edited by S. Doniger, 1962; THE DIALOGUE BETWEEN THEOLOGY AND PSYCHOLOGY, edited by P. Homans, 1968; THE NEW SHAPE OF PASTORAL THEOLOGY, edited by W. Oglesby, 1969; and CREATIVE MINISTRY, by H. Nouwen, 1970.

[8]Clinebell, who has been averaging close to a book per year since 1965, has focused on various aspects of mental health in numerous articles and chapters of books as well as his own volumes. His influence has also been extended through his lectures and seminars throughout this country and abroad and through his leadership of the American Association of Pastoral Counselors (1964-65).

[9]Note the assessment of Paul Pruyser, Director of the Department of Education at The Menninger Foundation: "The sizeable body of literature which has tried to come to grips with mental illness, even within psychiatry alone, will leave the reader aghast at the difficulties in defining it. The smaller body of literature devoted to statements about the nature of mental health is even more perplexing. The scientific language on health is more elusive than its terms for illness, and the popular language on health abounds with trite statements and quasi-pious phrases." "Five Edifying Discourses on Mental Illness and Health," PASTORAL PSYCHOLOGY, 17 (May, 1966), 9.

[10]Defining normality in statistical terms places undue emphasis on the average individual (numerical majority) while underestimating deviations from the norm (numerical

minorities), including such individuals as geniuses, nonconformists and the exceptionally healthy. Allport--"Personality: Normal and Abnormal," SOCIOLOGICAL REVIEW, 6 (December, 1958), 167-80--in an address delivered at the Fifth Interamerican Congress of Psychology in 1957, emphasized the importance of developing a significant concept of normality in terms of ethical standards. Presently, the stages of moral development research of Kohlberg and his associates appears to be providing the kind of new thrust for which Allport was searching.

[11] Allport, Rogers, Maslow, Skinner, Mowrer and Erikson are among those investigators who have attempted to specify partial or complete models of positive mental health.

INTRODUCTION

[1] Thomas Fawcett, THE SYMBOLIC LANGUAGE OF RELIGION (London: SCM, 1970).

[2] Fawcett presents a discerning study of the nature, development and use of religious language. His chapter on "Models" is particularly suitable for the purpose of this study, since his treatment of the employment of models in religion and science provides useful interpretive categories. It should be noted that Fawcett has drawn some of his categories from the studies of M. Black--MODELS AND METAPHORS (Ithaca: Cornell University, 1962), 219-43--and I. T. Ramsey --MODELS AND MYSTERY (London: Oxford University, 1946). Neither discussion, in the judgment of this author, is as useful to the present study as Fawcett's chapter. Black is preoccupied with the argument that models play an essential role in scientific research, and Ramsey is engaged with the thesis that scientific models entail uncertainty and mystery as do theological models.

[3] Rather than follow the procedure of footnoting every paragraph, the author here directs the reader to Fawcett's discussion in THE SYMBOLIC LANGUAGE OF RELIGION covering pages 69-94.

[4] The significance of this observation for further differentiating the control models of religion and science should not be overlooked. It means that the religious control model maintains a philosophical (metaphysical) or theological assumption about the fundamental nature of reality. When it is the Christian religion that is being referred to, as is the case in this study, the necessary theological assumption is that the God-man relationship is what is to be considered essential, concrete reality. When

this assumption is held as an exclusivistic claim or as a denial of the reality of the empirical world, theological reductionism is the result. The scientific control model, on the other hand, only necessarily maintains its assumption of the primacy of the concreteness of the empirical, objective world on a methodological level. When this assumption is transformed into a metaphysical assertion equating total reality with that which is verifiable by scientific method, the result is a reductionistic faith stance in the opposite direction from its theological counterpart.

CHAPTER I

[1]Cf. Joseph Swain, HARPER HISTORY OF CIVILIZATION (New York: Harper and Bros., 1958), II, 506-22.

[2]Cf. Edwin Gaustad, A RELIGIOUS HISTORY OF AMERICA (New York: Harper and Row, 1966), 214-17, 227-28.

[3]Cf. Ruth Caplan, PSYCHIATRY AND THE COMMUNITY IN NINETEENTH-CENTURY AMERICA (New York: Basic Books, 1969), 9-43.

[4]Cf. IBID., 47-9.

[5]Cf. IBID., 143-57.

[6]Cf. Martin Marty, RIGHTEOUS EMPIRE (New York: Dial, 1970), 112, 188-9.

[7]IBID., 190-3.

[8]IBID., 190-3, 215-20.

[9]Anton Boisen, "The Challenge to Our Seminaries," JOURNAL OF PASTORAL CARE (reprinted from the January 23, 1926 issue of CHRISTIAN WORK), 5 (Spring, 1951), 12.

[10]This is true in part because of the work of Boisen's students, but it also would appear to be the result of the setting (predominantly general and mental hospitals) of clinical pastoral educational programs.

[11]Cf. Charles Hopkins, THE RISE OF THE SOCIAL GOSPEL IN AMERICAN PROTESTANTISM, 1865-1915 (New Haven: Yale University, 1940), 3-7, 121-301.

[12]Cf. Marty, 208-9, 234-8.

[13]Cf. Lloyd Averill, AMERICAN THEOLOGY IN THE LIBERAL TRADITION (Philadelphia: Westminster, 1967), 13-22.

[14]Caplan, 298-301.

[15]Cf. Nina Ridenour, MENTAL HEALTH IN THE UNITED STATES (Cambridge: Harvard University, 1961), 1-3.

[16]Cf. IBID., 78.

[17]Cf. H. Wechsler, L. Solomon and B. Kramer (eds.), SOCIAL PSYCHOLOGY AND MENTAL HEALTH (New York: Holt, Rinehart and Winston, 1970), 9. Also see B. Braginsky, D. Braginsky and K. Ring, METHODS OF MADNESS (New York: Holt, Rinehart and Winston, 1969), 1-12.

[18]Anton Boisen, OUT OF THE DEPTHS (New York: Harper and Bros., 1960), 9.

[19]IBID., 39.

[20]IBID., 34.

[21]IBID., 25-6.

[22]IBID., 43-44, 46, 50.

[23]IBID., 47.

[24]E.g., see IBID., 51, 56-7, 68, 70, 89 and 114.

[25]Note the coincidence of the two sets of facts: (1) Boisen was excited about his discovery of Freudian psychology --see p. 18 of this study--yet he feared and backed away from entering psychoanalysis; (2) one way of understanding the psychodynamics and events of Boisen's life, some of which he admits he never understood, is to interpret his conflict as an unresolved oedipal complex that left the boy of seven simultaneously victorious and defeated. His deep sense of guilt, his sexual problem, his feeling that he was a failure, his idealizing his parents, his viewing Alice as a mother image, together with the symbolic content of his hallucinations could all be viewed as part of an oedipal-conflict pattern.

[26]Boisen OUT OF THE DEPTHS, 26.

[27]IBID., 27.

[28]The view of Henri Nouwen--"Anton T. Boisen and Theology Through Living Human Documents," PASTORAL PSYCHOLOGY, 19 (September, 1968), 57--that Boisen transferred his feelings for his father onto Alice is less likely in light of the fact that Boisen admits that Alice was a mother-image for him.

[29]Boisen attended the university where his father had taught and majored in his father's field. Boisen, OUT OF THE DEPTHS, 41.

[30]IBID., 56.

[31]IBID., 65.

[32]IBID., 65-110.

[33]IBID., 112. It should be noted that Thornton, in asserting that Boisen experienced six psychiatric episodes, does not draw a distinction between symptoms of abnormality and a psychotic break with reality. Cf. Thornton, PROFESSIONAL EDUCATION FOR THE MINISTRY, 55.

[34]Cf. Thornton, PROFESSIONAL EDUCATION FOR THE MINISTRY, 59, 81-92, 114-20.

[35]IBID., 143-52, 172-90.

[36]IBID., 178-9.

[37]Cf. IBID., 159-77.

[38]IBID., 45.

[39]Hall, Starbuck, Pratt and Leuba are the early investigators Boisen later included with Coe and James--see Anton Boisen, "Cooperative Inquiry in Religion," JOURNAL OF PASTORAL CARE, 5 (Spring, 1951), 23. Among the studies carried out by these investigators, those by Starbuck on conversion were considered by Boisen to be most relevant to his own work.

[40]George Coe, THE PSYCHOLOGY OF RELIGION (Chicago: University of Chicago, 1916), 233.

[41]IBID., 244.

[42]While Boisen himself was a liberal and agreed with Coe on many issues (including the unsatisfactory approach of fundamentalism to human need and the importance of education for responsible affirmative living), he was critical of liberals for having little understanding of and no message of salvation for the deeply troubled. Cf. Anton Boisen, "In Defense of Mr. Bryan," AMERICAN REVIEW, 3 (May-June, 1925), 326-7.

[43]Cf. George Coe, THE RELIGION OF A MATURE MIND (New York: Fleming H. Revell, 1902), 377-82.

[44]IBID., 384. (Note that Coe goes on to speak of "concrete evil"--pp. 389, 392-99).

[45]Anton Boisen, THE EXPLORATION OF THE INNER WORLD (Chicago: Willett and Clark, 1936), 93-4.

[46]Note, for instance, Boisen's comment regarding how resistant Starbuck had been to such a conclusion even after a psychiatrist had pointed out to him that his findings were relevant to the study of mental illness. IBID., 90-1.

[47]Cf. William James, THE VARIETIES OF RELIGIOUS EXPERIENCE (New York: Longmans and Green, 1915), 134, 162.

[48]IBID., 426.

[49]Boisen, EXPLORATION, 89.

[50]William James, THE PRINCIPLES OF PSYCHOLOGY (New York: Henry Holt, 1890), vi-vii.

[51]Cf. James, VARIETIES, 498-9.

[52]IBID., 512.

[53]Boisen, who had studied under Cabot at Harvard, was impressed with the research potential of Cabot's medical case-study approach. Cf. Boisen, JOURNAL OF PASTORAL CARE, 5 (Spring, 1951), 5, 11. Also see Boisen, OUT OF THE DEPTHS, 147.

[54]Cf. Boisen, EXPLORATION, 104-6.

[55]Cf. William James, PRAGMATISM (New York: Longmans and Green, 1907), 201; and John Dewey, "The Control of Ideas by

Facts," JOURNAL OF PHILOSOPHY, PSYCHOLOGY AND SCIENTIFIC METHODS, 4 (April 11, 1907), 200-3.

[56]William James, "The Pragmatic Method," JOURNAL OF PHILOSOPHY, PSYCHOLOGY AND SCIENTIFIC METHODS, 1 (December 8, 1904), 676-82.

[57]Note Dewey's movement toward such a position in his "Beliefs and Realities," PHILOSOPHICAL REVIEW, 15 (March, 1906), 128. Also see Dewey's statement of his more developed position in A COMMON FAITH (New Haven: Yale University, 1934), 20-3.

[58]Cf. Josiah Royce, "The Eternal and the Practical," PHILOSOPHICAL REVIEW, 13 (March, 1904), 115-8, 141-2.

[59]Cf. James, JOURNAL OF PHILOSOPHY, PSYCHOLOGY AND SCIENTIFIC METHODS, 1, 683-5; and John Dewey, "A Reply to Professor Royce's Critique of Instrumentalism," PHILOSOPHICAL REVIEW, 21 (January, 1912), 80-1.

[60]Boisen, JOURNAL OF PASTORAL CARE, 5 (Spring, 1951), 5, 12.

[61]In this author's view, Royce's PHILOSOPHY OF LOYALTY (New York: Macmillan, 1908) was an attempt to demonstrate the scope of his own pragmatic interests as well as his position that pragmatism, rather than being inconsistent with absolute idealism, is inadequate apart from such a context.

[62]IBID., 16-26.

[63]IBID., 118.

[64]"Loyalty" is such a key concept in Boisen's understanding of health that he defines the term in his appended glossary. Boisen, EXPLORATION, 304-5.

[65]James, VARIETIES, 175.

[66]Dewey, A COMMON FAITH, 13.

[67]Boisen, EXPLORATION, 96.

[68]While Royce was attempting to establish the necessity of positing Absolute Truth, Boisen was attempting to discern the socio-psychological nature of that process which, in his

view, is referred to abstractly as the God-man relationship in traditional theology.

[69]Boisen, OUT OF THE DEPTHS, 103.

[70]Cf. Boisen, EXPLORATION, 105, 212.

[71]Anton Boisen, PROBLEMS IN RELIGION AND LIFE (New York: Abingdon-Cokesbury, 1946), 157.

[72]IBID., 153, 157.

[73]Boisen, OUT OF THE DEPTHS, 134.

[74]E.g., see McDougall's treatment of Jung and Freud in PSYCHOANALYSIS AND SOCIAL PSYCHOLOGY (London: Methuen, 1936).

[75]Cf. C. Macfie Campbell, "On Recent Contributions to the Study of the Personality," PROBLEMS OF PERSONALITY, ed. by C. M. Campbell, ET AL. (New York: Harcourt and Brace, 1925), 68, 73-4.

[76]Cf. C. Macfie Campbell, HUMAN PERSONALITY AND THE ENVIRONMENT (New York: Macmillan, 1934), 205-47. Also cf. DESTINY AND DISEASE (London: Chapman and Hall, 1935), 197-201.

[77]E.g., McDougall's understanding of the continuity between the unconscious and conscious thought processes, the problem-solving nature of these thought processes--which he viewed as explaining sudden solutions of all types of problems, from math problems to religious conversions--the collective nature of highly organized societies, and the relevance of social evolution to individual development, all find expression in Boisen. Cf. PSYCHOLOGY (New York: Henry Holt, 1912), 213-35.

[78]Cf. Boisen, EXPLORATION, 102.

[79]Cf. IBID., 106-9.

[80]Cf. IBID., 106-7. Also see Carl Jung, TWO ESSAYS ON ANALYTICAL PSYCHOLOGY, trans. by H. and C. Baynes (London: Bailliere, Tindall and Cox, 1928), 25, 45, 50-2, 67-8. [Note that these essays first appeared in English eight years earlier--COLLECTIVE PAPERS ON ANALYTICAL PSYCHOLOGY, ed. by C. Long (Bailliere, Tindall and Cox, 1920).]

[81]It would appear that Boisen's study of Jung helped him to organize his own insights. His basic understanding of acute functional psychoses, it should be noted, is very similar to Jung's understanding of neuroses. Note also that Boisen introduced his important early publication on functional psychoses with a pertinent quote from Jung. See Anton Boisen, "Personality Changes and Upheavals Arising Out of the Sense of Personal Failure," AMERICAN JOURNAL OF PSYCHIATRY, 5 (April, 1926), 533.

[82]Cf. Boisen, EXPLORATION, 115.

[83]Cf. IBID., 115, 198, 302-3.

[84]Cf. IBID., 202-3.

[85]Cf. Boisen, AMERICAN JOURNAL OF PSYCHIATRY, 5, 533. Also cf. Harry S. Sullivan, "Schizophrenia: Its Conservative and Malignant Features," AMERICAN JOURNAL OF PSYCHIATRY, 4 (July, 1924), 77-91.

[86]When Boisen voiced his unpopular viewpoint at the 1928 meeting of the American Sociological Society, stating that he had found support for the traditional Christian doctrine that conviction of sin is the initial step in the process of salvation, Sullivan defended his position. Boisen, OUT OF THE DEPTHS, 166.

[87]Cf. William McDougall, MODERN MATERIALISM AND EMERGENT EVOLUTION (London: Methuen, 1929), 42-3; and Boisen, OUT OF THE DEPTHS, 201.

[88]For a brief summary of McDougall's position, see his MODERN MATERIALISM, 155-6.

[89]Cf. William White, "Higher Levels of Mental Integration," THE UNCONSCIOUS, A SYMPOSIUM, ed. by E. Dummer (New York: Alfred A. Knopf, 1928), 250.

[90]Boisen, EXPLORATION, 176.

[91]Cf. William Brown, CHRISTIAN THEOLOGY IN OUTLINE (New York: Charles Scribner's Sons, 1906, 6-15.

[92]E.g., see IBID., 76-7, 97-8.

[93]In CHRISTIAN THEOLOGY IN OUTLINE, Brown emphasizes the

importance of interpreting life in the light of its highest development (e.g., pp. 9-10, 76, 95), differentiating between the idea of God and God himself (e.g., pp. 30-1), recognizing the significance of psychology and especially social psychology for theology (e.g., pp. 94, 192, 248), correlating the Christian idea of God with the needs of the whole man (e.g., p. 129), and discerning the constructive function of the sinner's experience of punishment (e.g., pp. 294-5).

[94] Cf. Walter Rauschenbusch, A THEOLOGY FOR THE SOCIAL GOSPEL (New York: Macmillan, 1917), 27, 92-4.

[95] IBID., 57.

[96] Boisen, PROBLEMS, 140.

[97] Cf. Walter Rauschenbusch, CHRISTIANITY AND THE SOCIAL CRISIS (New York: Macmillan, 1907), 351-67.

[98] Cf. Rauschenbusch, A THEOLOGY, 31-130.

[99] Seward Hiltner, personal communication, March 21, 1972.

[100] IBID.

[101] Seward Hiltner, "Towards a Theology of Conversion in the Light of Psychology," PASTORAL PSYCHOLOGY, 17 (September, 1966), 36.

[102] IBID.

[103] Hiltner, personal communication.

[104] Hiltner took all three of his quarters under Boisen trained supervisors, his first two under Donald Beatty at Pittsburgh City Home and Hospitals, and his third as an assistant supervisor under Carroll Wise at Worcester State Hospital.

[105] Hiltner, personal communication.

[106] IBID.

[107] Seward Hiltner, "Boisen and Human Knowledge," PASTORAL PSYCHOLOGY, 2 (April, 1952), 9.

[108]Note that Hiltner also found Sullivan's methodological considerations helpful. He closely followed Sullivan's clarifying statements about the "interpersonal fields" which include the participant observer. Compare Seward Hiltner, PREFACE TO PASTORAL THEOLOGY (New York: Abingdon, 1958), 20, with Harry S. Sullivan, THE INTERPERSONAL THEORY OF PSYCHIATRY, ed. by H. Perry and M. Gawel (New York: W. W. Norton, 1953), 13-4.

[109]Seward Hiltner, "The Psychological Understanding of Religion," CROZER QUARTERLY, 24 (January, 1947), 30.

[110]Seward Hiltner, "Pastoral Theology and Psychology," PROTESTANT THOUGHT IN THE TWENTIETH CENTURY, ed. by A. Nash (New York: Macmillan, 1951), 192.

[111]Cf. Seward Hiltner, "Religion and Psychoanalysis," JOURNAL OF PASTORAL CARE, 4 (Spring-Summer, 1950), 34; and Seward Hiltner, "Psychoanalysis and Religion--the Search for Completeness," CHRISTIAN REGISTER, 135 (March, 1956), 15.

[112]Seward Hiltner, CHRISTIAN REGISTER, 15, 32. Also see Seward Hiltner, "Freud for the Pastor," PASTORAL PSYCHOLOGY, 5 (January, 1955), 43-7.

[113]Hiltner, CHRISTIAN REGISTER, 135, 32.

[114]Hiltner has noted the mixture of mechanistic and process thinking in Freud and viewed Freud's later work as moving toward a more modern process orientation. Seward Hiltner, "Psychiatric Understandings of Man: A Theological Appraisal," CHRISTIANITY AND WORLD REVOLUTION, ed. by E. Rian (New York: Harper and Row, 1963), 96.

[115]In this regard, some of Hiltner's interests have paralleled those of Gardner Murphy (A BIOSOCIAL APPROACH TO ORIGINS AND STRUCTURE. New York: Harper and Bros., 1947) and Andras Angyal (FOUNDATIONS FOR A SCIENCE OF PERSONALITY. New York: Commonwealth Fund, 1941).

[116]Cf. Ludwig von Bertalanffy, MODERN THEORIES OF DEVELOPMENT (London: Humphrey Milford, 1933), 129-76.

[117]Apparently Hiltner was introduced to Goldstein in the mid-forties through the Columbia University Seminar on Religion and Health of which Goldstein was a contributing member.

[118]Cf. Kurt Goldstein, THE ORGANISM (New York: American Book, 1939), 335-9 and 427-43.

[119]IBID., 339-40.

[120]E.g., IBID., 131.

[121]From the early forties, when he participated in a study group with Fromm, Tillich, Roberts and Bone among others--cf. "Toward an Ethical Conscience," JOURNAL OF RELIGION, 25 (January, 1945), 1--Hiltner has profited from the interdisciplinary dialogues that have taken place in the New York City area, most of which have been sponsored by Columbia University and Union Theological Seminary.

[122]Cf. Seward Hiltner, PASTORAL COUNSELING (Nashville: Abingdon-Cokesbury, 1949), 29, 263, 284.

[123]Cf. IBID., 176, 284.

[124]Harry Bone, "The Personality in Difficulties," CHRISTIANITY AND MENTAL HYGIENE, ed. by S. Hiltner, O. Rice and W. York (Committee on Religion and Health, Federal Council of the Churches of Christ in America, 1939), 6.

[125]Hiltner, CROZER QUARTERLY, 24, 30.

[126]Cf. Hiltner, CHRISTIAN REGISTER, 135, 15.

[127]Seward Hiltner, "Eric Fromm and Pastoral Psychology," PASTORAL PSYCHOLOGY, 6 (September, 1955), 12.

[128]Arthur McGiffert, Jr., "The Christian Doctrine of Man," CHRISTIANITY AND MENTAL HYGIENE, ed. by S. Hiltner, O. Rice, and W. York (Committee on Religion and Health, Council of the Churches of Christ in America, 1939), 4.

[129]IBID.

[130]Cf. Seward Hiltner, "David E. Roberts," PASTORAL PSYCHOLOGY, 6 (December, 1955), 10.

[131]Cf. David Roberts, "Tillich's Doctrine of Man," THEOLOGY OF PAUL TILLICH, ed. by C. Kegley and R. Bretall (THE LIBRARY OF LIVING THEOLOGY, vol. 1; New York: Macmillan, 1952), 130.

[132] E.g., David Roberts, PSYCHOTHERAPY AND A CHRISTIAN VIEW OF MAN (New York: Charles Scribner's Sons, 1950), 56-8.

[133] Hiltner, PREFACE, 230.

[134] Hiltner is aware of the fact that, though focusing on different tasks, he and Tillich share a common heritage from Schleiermacher. See, for instance, footnote 23 in his PREFACE, 225, and his "Paul Tillich and Pastoral Psychology," PASTORAL PSYCHOLOGY, 16 (December, 1965), 7.

[135] Hiltner's use of or reference to Tillich's categories in the early 1950's differs markedly from his use or reference to them in the early 1960's. E.g., cf. the following studies by Hiltner: "The New Concern of Recent Years," THE CHURCH AND MENTAL HEALTH, ed. by P. Maves (New York: Charles Scribner's Sons, 1953), 66; "The Christian as Psychologist," CHRISTIAN SCHOLAR (SOUNDINGS), 37 (September, 1954), 400; "Conclusion: The Dialogue on Man's Nature," THE NATURE OF MAN, ed. by S. Doniger (New York: Harper and Bros., 1962), 251; "Psychiatric Understandings of Man...," 97-8.

[136] Paul Tillich, "The Relation of Religion and Health: Historical Considerations and Theoretical Questions," REVIEW OF RELIGION, 10 (May, 1946), 355-6.

[137] Note the influence of Tillich's early criticism in Hiltner's "Salvation's Message About Health," INTERNATIONAL REVIEW OF MISSIONS, 57 (April, 1968).

[138] Cf. Seward Hiltner, "The Future of Christian Anthropology," THEOLOGY TODAY, 20 (July, 1963), 247.

[139] Hiltner, "Conclusion: The Dialogue...," 251.

[140] Hiltner, "Psychiatric Understandings of Man...," 97-8.

[141] Cf. Hiltner, PASTORAL PSYCHOLOGY, 16, 7-8; or Hiltner's more recent statement in his "Pastoral Psychology--After Paul Tillich," PASTORAL PSYCHOLOGY, 19 (February, 1968), 6.

[142] Seward Hiltner, "Letter to the Editor," PASTORAL PSYCHOLOGY, 4 (March, 1953), 62.

[143] Hiltner has traced this theme back to Darwin and Spencer. Cf. his "Darwin and Religious Development,"

JOURNAL OF RELIGION, 40 (October, 1960), 285.

[144] Note, for instance, the way Hiltner begins several chapters of his book SELF-UNDERSTANDING (New York: Charles Scribner's Sons, 1951) with quotes from Whitehead.

[145] Hiltner's use of the field theory model will be treated later in this study. Suffice it to note at this point that he merely employed an elementary form of field theory which he found useful in a different context and for a different purpose than that in and for which most other investigators have utilized it.

[146] Cf. James Lapsley, "A Conceptualization of Health in Psychiatry," BULLETIN OF THE MENNINGER CLINIC, 26 (July, 1962), 166. Hiltner has stated in a personal communication that he is indebted to Lapsley for introducing him to the fundamental concept.

[147] Howard Clinebell, personal communication, February 16, 1972.

[148] IBID.

[149] IBID.

[150] IBID.

[151] IBID.

[152] Howard Clinebell, personal communication, November 19, 1971.

[153] IBID.

[154] IBID.

[155] IBID.

[156] Clinebell, personal communication, February 16, 1972.

[157] Cf. Ernest Becker, THE REVOLUTION IN PSYCHIATRY: THE NEW UNDERSTANDING OF MAN (New York: Glencoe, 1964), 2-3, 10-11.

[158] Clinebell, personal communication, February 16, 1972.

[159]IBID.

[160]The way in which Clinebell has incorporated Tillich's theological categories is indicative of the significant difference between his approach to theology and that of both Boisen and Hiltner. Their different approaches will be treated at a later point in this study. Suffice it to state here that Clinebell's practical approach, focusing on communicating theology rather than doing theology, places him within the mainline pastoral care orientation as elaborated by Carroll Wise--THE MEANING OF PASTORAL CARE (New York: Harper and Row, 1966)--among others.

[161]Clinebell, personal communication, February 16, 1972.

[162]Carney Landis, "Psychotherapy and Religion," REVIEW OF RELIGION, 10 (May, 1946), 421.

[163]Frederick Bolman, Horace Friess and Otis Rice, "Religion and Health: A Group Inquiry," REVIEW OF RELIGION, 10 (May, 1946), 346.

[164]Clinebell, personal communications, February 16, 1972 and December 27, 1973.

[165]Frank Kimper, "Howard J. Clinebell, Jr.," PASTORAL PSYCHOLOGY, 13 (April, 1962), 66.

[166]Cf. Sullivan, INTERPERSONAL THEORY, 37-45.

[167]Cf. Boisen, AMERICAN JOURNAL OF PSYCHIATRY, 5, 532; and Boisen, EXPLORATION, 148.

[168]Sullivan, INTERPERSONAL THEORY, 40-3.

[169]Howard Clinebell, "The Local Church's Contributions to Positive Mental Health," COMMUNITY MENTAL HEALTH: THE ROLE OF CHURCH AND TEMPLE, ed. by H. Clinebell (Nashville: Abingdon, 1970), 48.

[170]Cf. Howard Clinebell, BASIC TYPES OF PASTORAL COUNSELING (Nashville: Abingdon, 1966), 7.

[171]Cf. William Glasser, REALITY THERAPY (New York: Harper and Row, 1965)--note that the Forward is written by Mowrer. Also cf. O. Hobart Mowrer, THE CRISIS IN PSYCHIATRY AND RELIGION (Princeton: Van Nostrand, 1961) and O. Hobart Mowrer, THE NEW GROUP THERAPY (Princeton: Van Nostrand,

1964).

[172]Cf. Clinebell, personal communication, November 19, 1971.

[173]Cf. Howard Clinebell, GROWTH COUNSELING--NEW TOOLS FOR CLERGY AND LAITY (with the collaboration of Charlotte Clinebell), a recorded eight-cassette course in two parts (Nashville: Abingdon, 1973-74).

[174]Cf. Glasser, 43-4.

[175]Clinebell, BASIC TYPES, 233.

[176]E.g., see Carroll Wise, RELIGION IN ILLNESS AND HEALTH (New York: Harper and Bros., 1942); Carroll Wise, PSYCHIATRY AND THE BIBLE (New York: Harper and Bros., 1956); Wayne Oates, RELIGIOUS FACTORS IN MENTAL ILLNESS (New York: Association, 1955); and Wayne Oates, THE RELIGIOUS DIMENSIONS OF PERSONALITY (New York: Association, 1957).

[177]E.g., see Paul Johnson, PSYCHOLOGY OF RELIGION (rev. and enl.; Nashville: Abingdon, 1959); Paul Johnson, PERSONALITY AND RELIGION (New York: Abingdon, 1957); Reuel Howe, MAN'S NEED AND GOD'S ACTION (Greenwich: Seabury, 1953); and Reuel Howe, THE MIRACLE OF DIALOGUE (New York: Seabury, 1963).

[178]Wayne Oates, PROTESTANT PASTORAL COUNSELING (Philadelphia: Westminster, 1962), 13, 38.

[179]Paul Johnson, PSYCHOLOGY OF RELIGION, 289-91.

[180]Clinebell, personal communication, December 27, 1973.

CHAPTER II

[1]Boisen, EXPLORATION, ix.

[2]Cf. IBID., 27.

[3]Cf. Clinebell, BASIC TYPES, 245.

[4]Boisen expressed this conviction in a letter to Norman Nash dated September 18, 1921. See OUT OF THE DEPTHS, 135.

[5] Boisen, EXPLORATION, 18.

[6] Boisen's investigation of this problem entailed study of mentally ill subjects and the autobiographical and other writings of renowned historical figures of the Christian faith. With regard to the former, he was fortunate to become related to a neuro-endocrine research project directed by Dr. Roy Hoskins of Harvard Medical School. Boisen's study included most of the 173 schizophrenic patients--he lacked data on several--involved in Hoskins' studies. Boisen's objective was to study the experience (particularly the ideation) and behavior of these patients from his social psychology of religion standpoint in an effort to test out his hypothesis. With regard to the latter, he selected historical men of faith who had unmistakable psycho-pathological features manifest in their religious experience and behavior, on the one hand, and who had been obviously successful in transcending their difficulties and making a significant contribution to their respective religious groups, on the other hand. Each group was to be studied in light of the other. Cf. IBID., 16-18, 59-60.

[7] Cf. IBID., 150-1, 275-8.

[8] Cf. IBID., 182-3, 191.

[9] Cf. IBID., 220-1.

[10] Hiltner, PREFACE, 20.

[11] Cf. PREFACE, 28, 217-19. According to Hiltner's schema, general theology consists of logic-centered branches, such as Biblical and doctrinal theology and operation-centered branches, including pastoral, evangelistic and ecclesiastical theology.

[12] The shepherding perspective, as Hiltner defines it, consists of healing, sustaining and guiding. Since health and salvation are treated under healing, attention will be focused primarily on Hiltner's understanding of that aspect of shepherding.

[13] Hiltner, PREFACE, 98.

[14] IBID., 99-100.

[15] Hiltner maintains, it should be noted, that his field theory model is correct "in a preliminary way." Cf.

personal communication, March 21, 1972. It should be further noted that, in contrast to Thomas Oden's critical assessment --see CONTEMPORARY THEOLOGY AND PSYCHOTHERAPY (Philadelphia: Westminster, 1967)--Paul Mickey's evaluation of his theological position--see "Is There a 'Theology' in Seward Hiltner's Pastoral Theology?," PASTORAL PSYCHOLOGY, 21 (October, 1970)--has not discouraged Hiltner from assuming this posture.

[16]Cf. Clinebell, MENTAL HEALTH, 18.

[17]IBID.

[18]Howard Clinebell, "Introduction: The Community Mental Health Revolution--Challenge to Churches and Temples." COMMUNITY MENTAL HEALTH: THE ROLE OF CHURCH AND TEMPLE, ed. by H. Clinebell (Nashville: Abingdon, 1970), 14.

[19]The way Boisen employs "religion" as a general term will be discussed at a later point in this study. It should be noted here that Boisen was predominantly interested in Protestant Christianity which he viewed as the highest form in the evolution of religion, yet itself in danger of losing sight of its own nature and mission. Cf. EXPLORATION, 180, and RELIGION IN CRISIS, 185-91, 210-11, 245.

[20]Nouwen, PASTORAL PSYCHOLOGY, 50-1.

[21]Cf. Boisen, RELIGION IN CRISIS, 201-2.

[22]Note especially his tendency to avoid the use of "empirical theology"--the difficulties with his understanding of which will be brought out in later sections of this study--while still promoting the significance of empirical study for the task of the theologian. Cf. IBID., 189-90.

[23]One of the basic questions raised throughout Hiltner's early study was the nature and relation of health and salvation--e.g., see RELIGION AND HEALTH (New York: Macmillan, 1943), 23, 96, 101.

[24]Hiltner's most recent volume, entitled THEOLOGICAL DYNAMICS (Nashville: Abingdon, 1972), is indicative of his maturity as a pastoral theologian.

[25]Social change--cf. Howard Clinebell and Harvey Seifert, PERSONAL GROWTH AND SOCIAL CHANGE (Philadelphia: Westminster, 1969), and PEOPLE DYNAMIC (New York: Harper and Row, 1972)--and leadership skills--cf. Growth Counseling, part I, tape 1,

side B--are among his most recent interests.

[26]Boisen employed the term "empirical" in order to convey that, in his view, his theological conclusions were scientifically objective, concrete and sound. For the sake of clarity, from here on the author will use quotation marks with empirical and refer to Boisen's "empirical" theology as functional or clinical-phenomenological theology.

[27]Cf. Boisen, EXPLORATION, 198-200.

[28]Hiltner has maintained the process-oriented position that general theological statements are intellectual abstractions which are significant as long as they are not confused with the actual underlying processes. Cf. PREFACE, 217, and Paul Maves (ed.), THE CHURCH AND MENTAL HEALTH (New York: Charles Scribner's Sons, 1953), 74.

[29]Cf. Hiltner, PREFACE, 26-9, 56.

[30]Cf. IBID., 89-100.

[31]Cf. Hiltner, INTERNATIONAL REVIEW OF MISSIONS, 157-63. Also see "The Bible Speaks to the Health of Man," in CHURCH AND SOCIETY, 61 (March-April, 1971), 5-10.

[32]Hiltner makes it quite clear that pastoral theology as all branches of theology, has access to "the common currencies of the faith." PREFACE, 21, 26.

[33]Cf. Howard Clinebell, MENTAL HEALTH THROUGH CHRISTIAN COMMUNITY (New York: Abingdon, 1965), 16-25.

[34]IBID., 28-9.

[35]Cf. Clinebell, BASIC TYPES, 17, 19.

[36]It should be noted that Clinebell emphasizes his neoliberal Christian metaphysical position, rather than the theologies clustered about that position, in order to avoid inferring that there is only one adequate theology from the standpoint of mental health. Cf. MENTAL HEALTH, 28, 43.

[37]Based on his own experience as well as studies, Boisen pointed out that mentally ill persons often maintain that their hallucinatory ideas are authoritative solely on the basis of the mystical way in which their ideas have come to them. Cf. EXPLORATION, 117, 169-70. See also Boisen's

astute observation regarding the "ideation of primitive peoples," 192.

[38]Cf. IBID., 38-48.

[39]This interpretation is not intended to be a thorough description of Boisen's understanding of the therapeutic relationship. Rather it is intended to be a general description from the perspective of that which is central to Boisen's operational method of investigation. Cf. IBID., 151-2, 245.

[40]It should be kept in mind that Boisen was studying those persons who suffered with the same general type of mental illness he himself had experienced.

[41]Boisen only carried out "intensive therapeutic work" with "some cases." EXPLORATION, 17.

[42]E.g., in his autobiography, Boisen describes his discovery of the objective cause of his cross-on-the-moon delusion as "a big help toward recovery." OUT OF THE DEPTHS, 100-1.

[43]EXPLORATION, 16-7.

[44]Note that, in Hiltner's view, the shepherding person need not be a pastor. PREFACE, 37-9.

[45]IBID., 24.

[46]IBID., 220.

[47]IBID., 115.

[48]Cf. Hiltner, INTERNATIONAL REVIEW OF MISSIONS, 159, 161-3.

[49]Note Clinebell's ego-oriented understanding of the participant-observer process. E.g., see BASIC TYPES, 193-5, 235-9.

[50]The form referred to is the relationship-oriented form of pastoral counseling, and the context referred to is the religious context.

[51]Cf. Clinebell, BASIC TYPES, 52, 249, 255.

[52]Cf. IBID., 254-5.

[53]The corollary of this assumption is that only those fields dealing with abstractions, such as theology and philosophy, make use of models.

[54]E.g., note Boisen's normative reference to religion as "true religion" on the basis of its essential function. Cf. EXPLORATION, 213.

[55]Boisen apparently assumed that all emergents have essential, positive functions which it is the task of astute observation and/or experimentation to expose. Note that Boisen views God as "Intelligence" in his own personal faith position. EXPLORATION, 299.

[56]While Clinebell himself has never presented a diagram of the way he conceives the nature and relation of mental and spiritual health, he has concurred with the author's view that such a diagram, when viewed as a longitudinal cross-section of a sphere, is the most adequate way of representing his model. See personal communication, August 9, 1974.

CHAPTER III

[1]Personality, according to Boisen, "includes the temperamental and intellectual traits as well as the integration of belief, attitude and action...." EXPLORATION, 302.

[2]IBID.

[3]"Loyalty," as defined by Boisen, means "an accepted identification with some person or group." IBID., 304.

[4]IBID., 99-101.

[5]Cf. IBID., 92.

[6]Cf. IBID., 100.

[7]Hiltner, INTERNATIONAL REVIEW OF MISSIONS, 165.

[8]Cf. Clinebell (ed.), COMMUNITY MENTAL HEALTH, 52-56.

[9]Though Clinebell has recognized the adaptability of his

general model for Western religious and secular groups, the author is focusing on Clinebell's (Christian) pastoral psychological and theological understanding of his model. Note, for example, that he states: "Attention to upreach growth is just as vital in a school or secular group as in church or temple." PEOPLE DYNAMIC, 8.

[10]The one exception to this pattern is the discussion of Hiltner's second model. Since his second model is corrective of the first, to avoid being repetitious, only that material which distinguishes it from the first is treated.

[11]Cf. Boisen, EXPLORATION, 57.

[12]Cf. IBID., 148-50.

[13]Cf. IBID., 57, 81-2, 290.

[14]Cf. IBID., 162, 171-2, 199.

[15]Cf. IBID., 290.

[16]IBID., 196.

[17]IBID., 209.

[18]IBID., 175-6, 211-12.

[19]Both forms of sin, of course, entail both components. The question is whether one follows the route of predominantly inner conflict with self or predominantly external conflict with society. The former will be referred to as the internal-external form, and the latter as the external-internal form.

[20]Cf. EXPLORATION, 144, 201-2.

[21]Cf. IBID., 173, 201.

[22]IBID., 209.

[23]Hiltner, PREFACE, 94.

[24]Cf. Hiltner, "Toward an Ethical Conscience," 1-9.

[25]Hiltner, PREFACE, 110-11.

[26]IBID., 100.

[27]Cf. Seward Hiltner, THE CHRISTIAN SHEPHERD (New York: Abingdon, 1959), 23.

[28]Hiltner, INTERNATIONAL REVIEW OF MISSIONS, 162.

[29]IBID., 162-3.

[30]In Hiltner's analysis, by "person" is meant the Jewish concept of the unity of the organism implicit within his first model.

[31]Hiltner, INTERNATIONAL REVIEW OF MISSIONS, 159.

[32]IBID., 162.

[33]Cf. IBID., 165-6.

[34]Cf. IBID., 166, 169.

[35]Clinebell, MENTAL HEALTH, 48 and "Ego Psychology and Pastoral Counseling," PASTORAL PSYCHOLOGY, 14 (February, 1963), 26.

[36]Clinebell, "Ego Psychology and Pastoral Counseling," 28.

[37]Cf. Clinebell, BASIC TYPES, 144.

[38]IBID., 46.

[39]IBID.

[40]IBID., 280.

[41]Boisen did not use the terms "primary process" and "secondary process." The author employs these terms in order to underscore one of the ways in which Boisen was attempting to counter the Freudian position.

[42]Boisen, EXPLORATION, 174-5.

[43]IBID.

[44] IBID., 174, 176.

[45] Boisen notes: "The Freudian doctrine that the conscience is the product of the parental influences seems to me frequently to miss the point that the parent is merely the representative of something beyond himself." IBID., 174.

[46] IBID., 175.

[47] IBID., 178, 290.

[48] IBID., 144, 149, 196.

[49] What Boisen found in relation to schizophrenic patients was that those who had reacted with panic during and after the threat of psychotic onset had experienced a religious upswing in ideation and behavior. He found the same thing to be true for historical figures prior to and following religious conversion experiences. On the other hand, those patients who had either given up and drifted into psychosis or who had evaded the danger by delusional misinterpretation had shown a decline in religious concern prior to onset and afterward. In brief, only those who were apparently attempting to do something about the danger of their situation experienced an increase in religious concern. Cf. IBID., 53-4.

[50] Note Boisen's statement that "ideals or norms of perfection do not exist for themselves alone. They have a personal reference and are functions of that which we conceive to be the highest loyalty." "Christian Perfectionism," CHICAGO THEOLOGICAL SEMINARY REGISTER, 24 (January, 1934), 12.

[51] IBID., 176.

[52] IBID., 177.

[53] Cf. IBID., 54-6. Also see Boisen, "The Therapeutic Significance of Anxiety," JOURNAL OF PASTORAL CARE, 5 (Summer, 1951), 1-2.

[54] Cf. Boisen, EXPLORATION, 38, 39, 139, 204.

[55] Cf. IBID., 53, 212.

[56] Cf. IBID., 210-2.

[57]Cf. IBID., 153, 173-4.

[58]With regard to his historical cases, Boisen points out that "a sense of union with the Greater-than-self is characteristic. In them it becomes ... the foundation of a successful reorganization and transformation of the personality." IBID., 80. His meaning is later specified: "The ideal self, the super-ego, or whatever name one may prefer to use thus becomes the new center of the personality." IBID., 203.

[59]IBID., 285.

[60]Hiltner prefers to employ the term "healing" rather than "health." The former is clearly a process term, while the latter tends to connote a static state. When Hiltner does use the term "health," he means it in the dynamic sense of the healing process.

[61]Hiltner, PREFACE, 90.

[62]Cf. IBID., 89-90.

[63]Seward Hiltner, "Religious Development," PASTORAL PSYCHOLOGY, 7 (May, 1956), 8.

[64]IBID.; see also Seward Hiltner, "Darwin and Religious Development," 282, 285.

[65]Hiltner, PREFACE, 91, 93.

[66]Cf. IBID., 91-2.

[67]Cf. IBID., 92-3.

[68]Cf. IBID., 92, 95-6.

[69]Cf. IBID., 98-9.

[70]IBID., 95.

[71]Cf. IBID., 94-95.

[72]Cf. IBID., 95-8.

[73]IBID., 97-8.

[74]IBID., 99.

[75]Note that Hiltner's tendency to over-differentiate causes problems for him. On the one hand, he has differentiated between the healing and sustaining aspects of shepherding on the basis of whether or not the total situation is capable of change, and on the other hand, as in his illustration of the Parkinsonian, he clearly implies that it is the healing power resulting from responsible decision-making that, though the disease may not be thereby reversed, enables the organism to do whatever is possible to slow down the progress of the disease. Cf. IBID., 97, 116.

[76]IBID., 100.

[77]Cf. IBID.

[78]IBID., 101.

[79]Hiltner, INTERNATIONAL REVIEW OF MISSIONS, 159.

[80]Hiltner states that "the crux of the modern assumption is necessary attention to individuality, which is a proper working out of the biblical intent." IBID., 168.

[81]Cf. IBID., 160.

[82]IBID., 166.

[83]IBID., 160.

[84]Cf. IBID., 166-7.

[85]IBID., 167.

[86]As will become clear, the will-to-relate, motivated by the existential nature of man's reality-oriented being in the world, is fully understood as a psycho-socio-religious bridge concept.

[87]Cf. Clinebell, BASIC TYPES, 18.

[88]Cf. Clinebell, MENTAL HEALTH, 147.

[89]Cf. IBID., 200-2.

[90]IBID., 203. Note that Clinebell means love in all relationship dimensions, including "loving interaction with nature." BASIC TYPES, 251.

[91]Cf. Clinebell, BASIC TYPES, 249.

[92]IBID., 251.

[93]Clinebell, MENTAL HEALTH, 48.

[94]Clinebell, BASIC TYPES, 254.

[95]Cf. IBID., 146-7, 261.

[96]Cf. Clinebell, MENTAL HEALTH, 41.

[97]Cf. IBID., 52-3.

[98]Cf. IBID., 17.

[99]IBID., 17.

[100]Clinebell, PEOPLE DYNAMIC, 8.

[101]Clinebell (ed.), COMMUNITY MENTAL HEALTH, 48.

CHAPTER IV

[1]Note that in RELIGION IN CRISIS AND CUSTOM, Boisen makes explicit his criteria for distinguishing superior from inferior religious beliefs: consistency, continuity, social acceptance and social consequences. Cf. 186-8.

[2]Boisen, EXPLORATION, 183-9.

[3]Cf. IBID., 131, 186-7.

[4]IBID., 177.

[5]IBID., 299.

[6]Note Mickey's observation: "Hiltner's appeal to the common currency may well have been a kind of theological smoke screen behind which he, and the other pastoral

theologians, found freedom to get on with their work of pastoral care and counseling." PASTORAL PSYCHOLOGY, 29.

[7]During Hiltner's pre-PREFACE stage, he referred to the significance of Tillich's ontological approach to the God question--"Psychiatry and Thoughts on God," BULLETIN OF THE MENNINGER CLINIC, 19 (November, 1955), 220-2. Though one would expect to find Hiltner, once he had begun developing his own process theological orientation, employing some formulation of God in terms of Divine Process, Creativity or Becoming, this has not been the case. He apparently has resisted moving in this direction, perhaps because on this crucial issue Hiltner concurs with Tillich's position that form precedes dynamics. That is to say, when it comes to the issue of the nature of God in the God-man relationship, Being Itself precedes Becoming. It should further be noted that while Hiltner continues his silence on this issue in his recent THEOLOGICAL DYNAMICS, he does mention the possibility of a sequel in which the God question will be treated. Cf. 15.

[8]See Chapter I, fn. 25.

[9]Superego-oriented assimilation is a delimiting concept which promotes repression rather than actual integration, for moral ideals rather than actual reality-oriented needs determine what may and may not be acceptable aspects of the self.

This being the case, it is not surprising to find Boisen puzzling over the reason for his lack of therapeutic results. Granted he was working with extremely sick or psychotic persons. Nevertheless, his mixture of wholeness-centered therapeutic approaches with perfection-fostering relating apparently interfered with positive therapeutic movement on the part of his counselees. As sensitive as Boisen was to the importance of maintaining a non-judgmental posture and communicating forgiveness in pastoral counseling, his own difficulty with self-acceptance and capacity to form close relationships suggest that his insights pertaining to pastoral counseling were operationally deficient. Note, for instance, Boisen's conveyance of his tendency to over-identify with his counselees. Cf. EXPLORATION, 114-5, 200, 267-8.

[10]Hiltner, PREFACE, 99.

[11]IBID., 93.

[12]The author will focus on Hiltner's publications during the early 1960's, those years apparently representing the heat of the battle.

[13]Seward Hiltner, "Clinical and Theological Notes on Responsibility," JOURNAL OF RELIGION AND HEALTH, 2 (October, 1962), 13.

[14]Hiltner, "Conclusion: The Dialogue...," 241.

[15]IBID., 251.

[16]IBID., 256.

[17]Hiltner, "Psychiatric Understandings of Man...," 95.

[18]IBID., 98.

[19]Cf. Seward Hiltner and Lowell Colston, THE CONTEXT OF PASTORAL COUNSELING (Nashville: Abingdon, 1961), 29-31.

[20]Cf. Hiltner, THEOLOGY TODAY, 247, 254.

[21]IBID., 254.

[22]IBID., 255.

[23]Hiltner, CHRISTIAN ADVOCATE, 8.

[24]IBID.

[25]IBID.

[26]Cf. Mickey, PASTORAL PSYCHOLOGY, 27-32.

[27]Note that during the period in which he was most actively engaged in defending his first model, Hiltner clarified the fact that he recognizes the significance of both aspects of mental health. Cf. CHRISTIAN ADVOCATE, 7.

[28]Cf. Boisen, EXPLORATION, 209-11, 268.

[29]Hiltner, PREFACE, 222.

[30]It is not insignificant to note that from this pastoral psychological and theological perspective, God is viewed as Perfect Wholeness, i.e., perfectly free to love man unconditionally.

[31] Logistically, of course, in an analysis such as this, one must either treat form and dynamics together or treat them separately, one or the other necessarily first.

[32] "Self-identity" is employed to characterize the whole personality as organismic-self-in-process-of-becoming.

BIBLIOGRAPHY

Allport, Gordon. "Personality: Normal and Abnormal," SOCIOLOGICAL REVIEW, 6 (December, 1958), 167-80.

Angyal, Andras. FOUNDATIONS FOR A SCIENCE OF PERSONALITY. New York: Commonwealth Fund, 1941.

Averill, Lloyd. AMERICAN THEOLOGY IN THE LIBERAL TRADITION. Philadelphia: Westminster, 1967.

Becker, Ernest. THE REVOLUTION IN PSYCHIATRY: THE NEW UNDERSTANDING OF MAN. New York: Glencoe, 1964.

Black, Max. MODELS AND METAPHORS. Ithaca: Cornell University, 1962.

Boisen, Anton. "The Challenge to Our Seminaries," JOURNAL OF PASTORAL CARE, 5 (Spring, 1951), 8-12.

______________. "Christian Perfectionism," THE CHICAGO THEOLOGICAL SEMINARY REGISTER, 24 (January, 1934), 10-13.

______________. "Cooperative Inquiry in Religion," JOURNAL OF PASTORAL CARE, 5 (Spring, 1951), 17-26.

______________. THE EXPLORATION OF THE INNER WORLD. Chicago: Willett, Clark and Co., 1936.

______________. "Freud, Jung, and Fromm," PASTORAL PSYCHOLOGY, 2 (September, 1951), 52-54.

______________. "In Defense of Mr. Bryan," AMERICAN REVIEW, 3 (May, 1925), 323-38.

______________. OUT OF THE DEPTHS. New York: Harper and Bros., 1960.

______________. "Personality Changes and Upheavals Arising Out of the Sense of Personal Failure," AMERICAN JOURNAL OF PSYCHIATRY, 5 (April, 1926), 531-51.

______________. "The Present Status of William James' Psychology of Religion," JOURNAL OF PASTORAL CARE, 7 (Fall, 1953), 155-57.

______________. PROBLEMS IN RELIGION AND LIFE. New York: Abingdon-Cokesbury, 1946.

Boisen, Anton. RELIGION IN CRISIS AND CUSTOM. New York: Harper and Bros., 1945.

______________. "The Therapeutic Significance of Anxiety," JOURNAL OF PASTORAL CARE, 5 (Summer, 1951), 1-11.

Bolman, Frederick, Friess, Horace and Rice, Otis. "Religion and Health: A Group Inquiry," REVIEW OF RELIGION, 10 (May, 1946), 341-47.

Bone, Harry. "The Personality in Difficulties," CHRISTIANITY AND MENTAL HYGIENE. Ed. by S. Hiltner, O. Rice and W. York. Report of the Conference at Greenwich, Connecticut in August, 1938. Committee on Religion and Health, Federal Council of the Churches of Christ in America, 1939, 1-4, 6-9, 11-14.

Braginsky, Benjamin, Braginsky, Dorothea and Ring, Kenneth. METHODS OF MADNESS. New York: Holt Rinehart and Winston, 1969.

Brown, William. CHRISTIAN THEOLOGY IN OUTLINE. New York: Charles Scribner's Sons, 1906.

Campbell, C. Macfie. DESTINY AND DISEASE. London: Chapman and Hall, 1935.

______________. HUMAN PERSONALITY AND THE ENVIRONMENT. New York: Macmillan, 1934.

______________. "On Recent Contributions to the Study of the Personality." PROBLEMS OF PERSONALITY. Edited by C. M. Campbell, H. S. Langfield, W. McDougall, A. A. Roback and E. W. Taylor. New York: Harcourt, Brace and Co., 1925, 65-75.

Caplan, Ruth. PSYCHIATRY AND THE COMMUNITY IN NINETEENTH-CENTURY AMERICA. New York: Basic Books, 1969.

Clinebell, Howard. BASIC TYPES OF PASTORAL COUNSELING. Nashville: Abingdon, 1966.

Clinebell, Howard and Clinebell, Charlotte. THE INTIMATE MARRIAGE. New York: Harper and Row, 1970.

Clinebell, Howard. "Ego Psychology and Pastoral Counseling," PASTORAL PSYCHOLOGY, 14 (February, 1963), 26-36.

______________. GROWTH COUNSELING--NEW TOOLS FOR CLERGY AND LAITY. (With the collaboration of Charlotte Clinebell) A recorded eight-cassette course in two parts. Nashville: Abingdon, 1973-74.

Clinebell, Howard. "The Local Church's Contributions to Positive Mental Health," COMMUNITY MENTAL HEALTH: THE ROLE OF CHURCH AND TEMPLE. Ed. by H. Clinebell. Nashville: Abingdon, 1970, 46-56.

_______________. MENTAL HEALTH THROUGH CHRISTIAN COMMUNITY. New York: Abingdon, 1965.

_______________. "The Next Twenty Years in Pastoral Counseling," PASTORAL PSYCHOLOGY, 21 (February, 1970), 28-35.

_______________. THE PEOPLE DYNAMIC. New York: Harper and Row, 1972.

_______________. Personal Communication. December 27, 1973.

_______________. Personal Communication. February 16, 1972.

_______________. Personal Communication. November 19, 1971.

Clinebell, Howard and Seifert, Harvey. PERSONAL GROWTH AND SOCIAL CHANGE. Philadelphia: Westminster, 1969.

Coe, George. PSYCHOLOGY OF RELIGION. Chicago: University, 1916.

_______________. RELIGION OF A MATURE MIND. New York: Fleming H. Revell, 1902.

Dewey, John. "Beliefs and Realities," PHILOSOPHICAL REVIEW, 15 (March, 1906), 113-29.

_______________. A COMMON FAITH. New Haven: Yale University, 1934.

_______________. "The Control of Ideas by Facts," JOURNAL OF PHILOSOPHY, PSYCHOLOGY AND SCIENTIFIC METHODS, 4 (April 11, 1907), 197-203.

_______________. "A Reply to Professor Royce's Critique of Instrumentalism," PHILOSOPHICAL REVIEW, 21 (January, 1912), 69-81.

Dicks, Russell. TOWARD HEALTH AND WHOLENESS. New York: Macmillan, 1960.

Fawcett, Thomas. THE SYMBOLIC LANGUAGE OF RELIGION. London: SCM, 1970.

Gaustad, Edwin. A RELIGIOUS HISTORY OF AMERICA. New York: Harper and Row, 1966.

Glasser, William. REALITY THERAPY. New York: Harper and Row, 1965.

Golstein, Kurt. ORGANISM. New York: American Book, 1939.

Hiltner, Seward. "The Bible Speaks for the Health of Man," CHURCH AND SOCIETY, 61 (March-April, 1971), 5-10, 48-53.

______________. "Boisen and Human Knowledge," PASTORAL PSYCHOLOGY, 2 (April, 1952), 9.

______________. "The Christian as Psychologist," CHRISTIAN SCHOLAR (SOUNDINGS), 37 (September, 1954), 396-401.

______________. THE CHRISTIAN SHEPHERD. New York: Abingdon, 1959.

______________. "Clinical and Theological Notes on Responsibility," JOURNAL OF RELIGION AND HEALTH, 2 (October, 1962), 7-20.

Hiltner, Seward and Colston, Lowell. THE CONTEXT OF PASTORAL COUNSELING. Nashville: Abingdon, 1961.

Hiltner, Seward. "Conclusion: The Dialogue on Man's Nature," THE NATURE OF MAN. Ed. by S. Doniger. New York: Harper and Bros., 1962, 237-61.

______________. "Darwin and Religious Development," JOURNAL OF RELIGION, 40 (October, 1960), 282-95.

______________. "David E. Roberts," PASTORAL PSYCHOLOGY, 6 (December, 1955), 9-11.

______________. "Erich Fromm and Pastoral Psychology," PASTORAL PSYCHOLOGY, 6 (September, 1955), 11-12..

______________. "Freud for the Pastor," PASTORAL PSYCHOLOGY, 5 (January, 1955), 41-57.

______________. "Freud, Psychoanalysis, and Religion," PASTORAL PSYCHOLOGY, 7 (November, 1956), 9-21.

______________. "The Future of Christian Anthropology," THEOLOGY TODAY, 20 (July, 1963), 242-57.

______________. "Letter to the Editor," PASTORAL PSYCHOLOGY, 4 (March, 1953), 60-62.

______________. "Mental Health and Spiritual Wholeness," THE CHRISTIAN ADVOCATE, VII, 16, 7-8.

______________. "The New Concern of Recent Years," THE CHURCH AND MENTAL HEALTH. Ed. by P. Maves. New York: Charles Scribner's Sons, 1953, 61-74.

Hiltner, Seward. PASTORAL COUNSELING. Nashville: Abingdon-Cokesbury, 1949.

_______________. "Pastoral Psychology--After Paul Tillich," PASTORAL PSYCHOLOGY, 19 (February, 1968), 5-6.

_______________. "Pastoral Psychology and the Future," PASTORAL PSYCHOLOGY, 21 (February, 1970), 3-7, 82.

_______________. "Pastoral Theology and Psychology," PROTESTANT THOUGHT IN THE TWENTIETH CENTURY. Ed. by A. Nash. New York: Macmillan, 1951, 181-99.

_______________. "Paul Tillich and Pastoral Psychology," PASTORAL PSYCHOLOGY, 16 (December, 1965), 5-10.

_______________. Personal Communication. March 21, 1972.

_______________. PREFACE TO PASTORAL THEOLOGY. New York: Abingdon, 1958.

_______________. "Psychiatric Understandings of Man: A Theological Appraisal," CHRISTIANITY AND WORLD REVOLUTION. Ed. by E. Rian. New York: Harper and Row, 1963, 87-105.

_______________. "Psychiatry and Thoughts on God," BULLETIN OF THE MENNINGER CLINIC, 19 (November, 1955), 217-26.

_______________. "The Psychological Understanding of Religion," CROZER QUARTERLY, 24 (January, 1947), 3-36.

_______________. "Psychoanalysis and Religion--the Search for Completeness," CHRISTIAN REGISTER, 138 (March, 1956), 14-15, 32-34.

_______________. RELIGION AND HEALTH. New York: Macmillan, 1943.

_______________. "Religion and Psychoanalysis," JOURNAL OF PASTORAL CARE, 4 (Spring-Summer, 1950), 32-42.

_______________. "Religious Development," PASTORAL PSYCHOLOGY, 7 (May, 1956), 7-8, 66.

_______________. "Salvation's Message About Health," INTERNATIONAL REVIEW OF MISSIONS, 57 (April, 1968), 157-74.

_______________. SELF-UNDERSTANDING. New York: Charles Scribner's Sons, 1951.

_______________. "The Social Self," PASTORAL PSYCHOLOGY, 9 (February, 1958), 7-8.

Hiltner, Seward. THEOLOGICAL DYNAMICS. Nashville: Abingdon, 1972.

_______________. "Toward an Ethical Conscience," JOURNAL OF RELIGION, 25 (January, 1945), 1-9.

_______________. "Towards a Theology of Conversion in the Light of Psychology," PASTORAL PSYCHOLOGY, 17 (September, 1966), 35-42.

Homans, Peter (ed.). THE DIALOGUE BETWEEN THEOLOGY AND PSYCHOLOGY. Chicago: University, 1968.

Hopkins, Charles. THE RISE OF THE SOCIAL GOSPEL IN AMERICAN PROTESTANTISM, 1865-1915. New Haven: Yale University, 1940.

Howe, Reuel. MAN'S NEED AND GOD'S ACTION. Greenwich: Seabury, 1953.

_______________. THE MIRACLE OF DIALOGUE. New York: Seabury, 1963.

James, William. "The Pragmatic Method," JOURNAL OF PHILOSOPHY, PSYCHOLOGY AND SCIENTIFIC METHODS, 1 (December 18, 1904), 673-87.

_______________. PRAGMATISM. New York: Longmans, Green, and Co., 1907.

_______________. PRINCIPLES OF PSYCHOLOGY. New York: Henry Holt and Co., 1890.

_______________. THE VARIETIES OF RELIGIOUS EXPERIENCE. Revised edition. New York: Longmans, Green, and Co., 1915.

Johnson, Paul. PERSONALITY AND RELIGION. New York: Abingdon, 1957.

_______________. PSYCHOLOGY OF RELIGION. Revised and enlarged. Nashville: Abingdon, 1959.

Jung, Carl G. COLLECTIVE PAPERS ON ANALYTICAL PSYCHOLOGY. Ed. by C. Long. London: Baillieve, Tindall and Cox, 1920.

_______________. TWO ESSAYS ON ANALYTICAL PSYCHOLOGY. Trans. by H. and C. Baynes. London: Baillieve, Tindall, and Cox, 1928.

Kimper, Frank. "Howard J. Clinebell, Jr.," PASTORAL PSYCHOLOGY, 13 (April, 1962), 4, 66.

Landis, Carney. "Psychotherapy and Religion," REVIEW OF RELIGION, 10 (May, 1946), 413-24.

Lapsley, James. "A Conceptualization of Health in Psychiatry," BULLETIN OF THE MENNINGER CLINIC, 26 (July, 1962), 161-77.

Marty, Martin. RIGHTEOUS EMPIRE. New York: Dial, 1970.

McDougall, William. MODERN MATERIALISM AND EMERGENT EVOLUTION. London: Methuen, 1929.

______________. PSYCHO-ANALYSIS AND SOCIAL PSYCHOLOGY. London: Methuen and Co., 1936.

______________. PSYCHOLOGY. New York: Henry Holt and Co., 1912.

McGiffert, Arthur. "The Christian Doctrine of Man," CHRISTIANITY AND MENTAL HYGIENE. Ed. by S. Hiltner, O. Rice and W. York. Report of the Conference at Greenwich, Connecticut in August, 1938. Committee on Religion and Health, Federal Council of the Churches of Christ in America, 1939, 4-6, 9-11, 14-17.

Mickey, Paul. "Is There a 'Theology' in Seward Hiltner's Pastoral Theology?," PASTORAL PSYCHOLOGY, 21 (October, 1970), 27-32.

Mowrer, O. Hobart. THE CRISIS IN PSYCHIATRY AND RELIGION. Princeton: Van Nostrand, 1961.

______________. THE NEW GROUP THERAPY. Princeton: Van Nostrand, 1964.

Murphy, Gardner. A BIOSOCIAL APPROACH TO ORIGINS AND STRUCTURE. New York: Harper and Bros., 1947.

Nouwen, Henry. "Anton T. Boisen and Theology Through Living Human Documents," PASTORAL PSYCHOLOGY, 19 (September, 1968), 49-63.

______________. CREATIVE MINISTRY. New York: Doubleday, 1971.

Oates, Wayne. PROTESTANT PASTORAL COUNSELING. Philadelphia: Westminster, 1962.

______________. THE RELIGIOUS DIMENSIONS OF PERSONALITY. New York: Association, 1957.

______________. RELIGIOUS FACTORS IN MENTAL ILLNESS. New York: Association, 1955.

Oates, Wayne. "Quintessential," CHRISTIAN CENTURY, 72 (November 16, 1955), 1339.

Oglesby, William (ed.). THE NEW SHAPE OF PASTORAL THEOLOGY. Nashville: Abingdon, 1969.

Pruyser, Paul. "Five Edifying Discourses on Mental Illness and Health," PASTORAL PSYCHOLOGY, 17 (May, 1966), 9-18.

Ramsey, Ian T. MODELS AND MYSTERY. London: Oxford University, 1964.

Rauschenbusch, Walter. CHRISTIANITY AND THE SOCIAL CRISIS. New York: Macmillan, 1907.

______________. A THEOLOGY FOR THE SOCIAL GOSPEL. New York: Macmillan, 1917.

Rickel, William, Tillich, Paul, Wise, Carroll, Millet, John, Dicks, Russell and Boisen, Anton. "Is Psychotherapy a Religious Process?," (A Reader's Forum), PASTORAL PSYCHOLOGY, 7 (March, 1956), 36-46.

Ridenour, Nina. MENTAL HEALTH IN THE UNITED STATES. Cambridge: Harvard University, 1961.

Roberts, David. PSYCHOTHERAPY AND A CHRISTIAN VIEW OF MAN. New York: Charles Scribner's Sons, 1950.

______________. "Tillich's Doctrine of Man," THEOLOGY OF PAUL TILLICH. Edited by C. Kegley and R. Bretall. Vol. 1 of LIBRARY OF LIVING THEOLOGY. New York: Macmillan, 1952, 108-31.

Royce, Josiah. "The Eternal and the Practical," PHILOSOPHICAL REVIEW, 13 (March, 1904), 113-142.

______________. PHILOSOPHY OF LOYALTY. New York: Macmillan, 1908.

Sullivan, Harry S. THE INTERPERSONAL THEORY OF PSYCHIATRY. Ed. by H. Perry and M. Gavrel. New York: W. W. Norton and Co., 1953.

______________. "Schizophrenia: Its Conservative and Malignant Features," AMERICAN JOURNAL OF PSYCHIATRY, 4 (July, 1924), 77-91.

Swain, Joseph. Vol. II: HARPER HISTORY OF CIVILIZATION. New York: Harper and Row, 1966.

Thornton, Edward. PROFESSIONAL EDUCATION FOR MINISTRY. Nashville: Abingdon, 1970.

Thornton, Edward. THEOLOGY AND PASTORAL COUNSELING. Englewood Cliffs: Prentice-Hall, 1964.

Tillich, Paul. "The Relation of Religion and Health: Historical Considerations and Theoretical Questions," REVIEW OF RELIGION, 10 (May, 1946), 349-84.

Von Bertallanffy, Ludwig. MODERN THEORIES OF DEVELOPMENT. London: Humphrey Milford, 1933.

Wechsler, Henry, Solomon, Leonard and Kramer, Bernard (eds.). SOCIAL PSYCHOLOGY AND MENTAL HEALTH. New York: Holt, Rinehart and Winston, 1970.

White, William. "Higher Levels of Mental Integration," THE UNCONSCIOUS, A SYMPOSIUM. Edited by E. Dummer. New York: Alfred A. Knopf, 1928.

Wise, Carroll. THE MEANING OF PASTORAL CARE. New York: Harper and Row, 1966.

_______________. PSYCHIATRY AND THE BIBLE. New York: Harper and Bros., 1956.

_______________. RELIGION IN ILLNESS AND HEALTH. New York: Harper and Bros., 1942.